# The End of Work

## Automation's Threat to Human Identity

MICHAEL MOKOBANE

Published by Michael Mokobane

# DEDICATION

To the workers whose hands, minds, and hearts have built
the world we live in—this book is for you.
To every individual facing uncertainty in the shadow of
automation, and to those redefining what it means to work
and thrive in a changing world—your resilience inspires us
all.
To my family, friends, and mentors—your unwavering belief
and support have given me the strength to explore these
complex challenges.
And to the next generation, may you find new ways to
reclaim purpose, meaning, and dignity in a world reshaped by
technology. The future belongs to those who dare to
reimagine it.

# CONTENTS

ACKNOWLEDGMENTS i

INTRODUCTION 1

1 The Fourth Industrial Revolution: AI, robotics, and beyond 9

2 Job displacement: Sectors most vulnerable to automation 15

3 The pace of change: Accelerating technological advancements 21

4 Global implications: The worldwide impact of automation 27

5 Identity crisis: The psychological impact of job loss 36

6 Social disintegration: Community and family structures under threat 42

7 Mental health concerns: Anxiety, depression, and isolation 48

8 Economic insecurity: The erosion of financial stability 54

9 Redefining work: Shifting perspectives on employment and purpose 62

10 Universal Basic Income (UBI): A potential solution? 67

11 Education and re-skilling: Preparing for an automated future 73

12 Entrepreneurship and innovation: New paths to economic empowerment 79

13 Policy responses: Government strategies for mitigating automation's impact 88

14 Corporate responsibility: Business leaders' role in managing change 94

15 Community initiatives: Local solutions for a global problem 102

16 Personal Resilience – Strategies for Adapting to an Uncertain Future 110

17 Summary of key findings and implications 118

18 Call to Action: Collective Responsibility for Shaping the Future 125

19 Epilogue: The Future of Human Identity in an Automated World 132

# ACKNOWLEDGMENTS

A special thank you to my family and friends for their unwavering support and encouragement. Your belief in me has been a constant source of strength. Your encouragement has been my guiding light throughout this journey. Finally, I extend my gratitude to the readers of this book—those who care deeply about the future of work and what it means to be human in an age of rapid technological change. It is my hope that this book inspires new conversations and encourages collective action to shape a future that values both innovation and humanity.

# INTRODUCTION

## Foreword: The Looming Crisis of Automation

The world stands on the brink of a new era—one defined by rapid technological advancements, where artificial intelligence (AI), robotics, and automation are reshaping industries, economies, and societies at an unprecedented pace. The arrival of these technologies has sparked both excitement and fear. On the one hand, automation offers the potential for increased efficiency, reduced costs, and innovation beyond what we thought possible. But on the other hand, it presents a daunting challenge: the displacement of millions of jobs, altering not just how we work but also who we are.

In South Africa, where unemployment remains one of the country's most pressing issues, automation introduces both opportunities and risks. While new technologies may offer solutions to boost productivity and improve service delivery, they also threaten industries such as mining, manufacturing, and retail—key sectors upon which many South Africans depend. Globally, similar anxieties are surfacing, as governments, businesses, and individuals grapple with the unsettling question: *What does the future of work look like when machines can do most of it?*

This book explores the deeper consequences of automation, going beyond the economic impact to examine the existential threat it poses to human identity. Work is not merely about earning a living—it is about meaning, structure, and belonging. When that disappears, what remains? Automation forces us to reconsider long-held ideas about productivity, purpose, and the role of human beings in a changing world. It asks us to rethink not just the future of jobs but the future of people.

## Understanding the Threat to Human Identity

Work has always been more than a means of survival; it is integral to how we define ourselves and engage with the world around us. Whether we labour in fields, operate machinery, manage businesses, or care for others, work provides a sense of routine, purpose, and accomplishment. It is deeply tied to identity—forming the backbone of our social structures and giving individuals a sense of belonging. In many societies, including South Africa, one's occupation often serves as a marker of status, pride, and contribution to the broader community.

However, the rise of automation challenges this fundamental relationship between work and identity. When machines and algorithms perform tasks once carried out by human hands and minds, the very nature of employment changes. Jobs that took decades to master, from factory work to financial analysis, are now automated with the press of a button. This shift raises profound questions: *Who are we if our work is no longer needed? What purpose will humans serve in a world where machines take over most functions?*

This book seeks to explore the human dimension of automation, a conversation often overshadowed by economic forecasts and technological developments. While much of the focus tends to be on job numbers—how many jobs will be lost or created—far less attention is given to the psychological, social, and emotional consequences of a society where meaningful work is scarce. For many people, employment is a source of identity, pride, and connection. Without it, they may face an existential crisis that impacts not only their personal wellbeing but also the cohesion of families and communities.

In a country like South Africa, where work has historically been tied to struggles for dignity and liberation, the threat of widespread job displacement takes on even greater significance. During apartheid, job opportunities for black South Africans were limited, and access to meaningful work became a symbol of equality and progress. Today, with high unemployment already a reality, automation poses a further risk to a fragile social fabric. This book asks: *How do we navigate this transition while preserving our sense of self and ensuring that no one is left behind?*

# Context: Historical Perspective on Work and Identity

Throughout history, work has been an essential part of human life, providing structure and meaning across cultures and societies. Early hunter-gatherer communities relied on shared labour to secure food and ensure survival. With the agricultural revolution, people began to cultivate crops, domesticate animals, and organise themselves around permanent settlements, giving rise to the division of labour and the development of professions.

The industrial revolution in the 18th and 19th centuries brought profound changes to how people worked. Factories replaced farms as the primary source of employment, and urbanisation saw large numbers of workers migrate to cities in search of better opportunities. With this shift came a new relationship between individuals and their jobs—work became not just a means of survival but also a source of personal identity and pride. Men and women identified themselves by their trades, from blacksmiths and tailors to engineers and teachers. In South Africa, the transition from agrarian to industrial labour was shaped by colonialism, segregation, and later apartheid, with economic opportunities restricted along racial lines.

The struggle for meaningful work was central to the liberation movements that sought to dismantle apartheid and create a society where every citizen could participate in the economy. For many black South Africans, the right to work was about more than just earning an income—it was a matter of dignity and equality. This legacy continues to shape how work is viewed in post-apartheid South Africa, where employment is not only a personal achievement but also a means of social upliftment and community development.

In recent decades, however, globalisation and technological advancements have disrupted traditional forms of work. Many jobs once considered stable—like mining, factory work, and clerical jobs—are now increasingly automated or outsourced. The digital revolution has given rise to new industries and opportunities, but it has also deepened economic inequalities, with some individuals thriving in high-tech sectors while others are left behind. South Africa, with its complex history and economic disparities, is particularly vulnerable to these disruptions.

The rise of automation marks the next chapter in this evolution. While previous technological shifts created new jobs even as they destroyed old ones, there is growing concern that this time might be different. Machines and algorithms are becoming increasingly capable of performing not just manual tasks but also cognitive work. As automation accelerates, the question becomes: *Will there be enough meaningful work left for humans? And if not, how do we redefine identity and purpose in a world where jobs are scarce?*

This book takes a close look at these issues,

exploring not only the challenges of automation but also the opportunities for reimagining work, identity, and purpose. It seeks to offer a roadmap for navigating this transition, focusing on the importance of resilience, innovation, and collective action. While the future may be uncertain, it is also full of possibility. By embracing change thoughtfully and proactively, we can create a world where technology serves humanity, not the other way around.

This introduction sets the stage for an exploration of the complex relationship between work, identity, and automation, with a particular focus on the South African context. The chapters that follow will delve deeper into the impact of technological change, offering insights into the human cost of automation and strategies for building a more inclusive, purposeful future.

# Part 1: Understanding The Rise of Automation

# 1 The Fourth Industrial Revolution: AI, robotics, and beyond

The world is in the midst of a transformation so profound that many compare it to the seismic shifts brought about by the first three industrial revolutions. The First Industrial Revolution saw the mechanisation of production through steam power. The Second brought mass production, powered by electricity and assembly lines, while the Third ushered in the digital era, introducing computers and automation into the workplace. But now, the Fourth Industrial Revolution, driven by artificial intelligence (AI), robotics, the Internet of Things (IoT), and big data, promises to change not just how we work but what it means to work at all. Unlike the revolutions before it, this one goes beyond machines assisting humans—now, machines are capable of learning, reasoning, and making decisions on their own.

At the heart of this revolution lies AI—an extraordinary advancement that allows machines to replicate complex human thought processes. What sets AI apart is its ability to analyse vast amounts of data, identify patterns, and make predictions far faster than humans ever could. Algorithms that power AI systems are being used across industries, from healthcare to finance, retail to agriculture. Machines no longer simply follow a set of instructions; they learn from their mistakes and improve continuously. AI-enabled software is managing stock portfolios, diagnosing illnesses, predicting consumer behaviour, and even driving cars. And with each passing day, the sophistication of these technologies grows.

Robotics, another key pillar of this revolution, has also advanced by leaps and bounds. Today's robots are not the clunky mechanical arms that characterised the early days of industrial automation. Modern robots are versatile, mobile, and equipped with sensory systems that allow them to adapt to changing environments. Autonomous drones monitor infrastructure and deliver goods, while robots are already being used in warehouses, logistics chains, and even hospitals. In South African factories, such as those in the automotive sector, robots have become integral to manufacturing processes, performing tasks that are repetitive or dangerous with speed and precision. As these machines become more capable, the need for human labour in routine and hazardous tasks is rapidly diminishing.

Yet, the Fourth Industrial Revolution is not just about individual technologies—it is about convergence. Robotics, AI, IoT, and 3D printing are interweaving to create new ecosystems of work. For example, smart factories are using AI-powered systems to anticipate equipment failures before they occur, ensuring that production lines remain uninterrupted. Agriculture is undergoing a transformation through the use of automated tractors, drone surveillance, and predictive software, helping farmers make better decisions while reducing human labour. In South Africa, the agricultural and manufacturing sectors, which have traditionally provided a large share of jobs, are now facing the difficult reality that fewer hands are needed as technology takes over many of the core functions.

This rapid technological progress holds immense potential but also carries significant risks. On one hand, automation and AI can lead to greater efficiency, reduced costs, and improved quality of life. Some experts argue that this revolution could create new kinds of jobs—ones we have not even imagined yet—just as previous revolutions did. They believe that while certain tasks will be automated, humans will always be needed for creative, emotional, and interpersonal roles. For example, while AI can diagnose diseases, human doctors are still essential for providing empathy and care to patients. But there is also a darker side to this revolution. The speed at which technology is advancing is leaving many people behind, particularly in developing countries like South Africa, where access to digital skills and resources remains unequal.

In South Africa, the potential for job displacement looms large. Traditional sectors such as mining, manufacturing, and retail—pillars of employment for decades—are particularly vulnerable to automation. Already, mining companies are introducing automated machinery to perform tasks previously handled by human workers, from drilling to monitoring safety conditions underground. Retailers are also adopting AI-powered systems, from automated checkouts to stock management software. As a result, jobs that were once the bedrock of communities, particularly in rural and low-income urban areas, are under threat. This shift creates a real risk of deepening unemployment and inequality in a country where many people already struggle to find work.

The rapid development of AI and robotics is also reshaping the nature of work itself. The concept of a "job for life" is disappearing, replaced by a gig economy that offers flexibility but little security. More workers are becoming freelancers or independent contractors, juggling multiple short-term jobs instead of holding a single stable position. While some embrace this freedom, others are left vulnerable, with little access to benefits such as pensions, healthcare, or paid leave. The gig economy has taken root in South Africa too, with companies like Uber and Mr D Food providing new forms of employment. But these roles are precarious, leaving many workers at the mercy of fluctuating demand and low wages.

The education system is also grappling with the implications of the Fourth Industrial Revolution. Schools and universities must prepare students for jobs that do not yet exist, requiring skills such as critical thinking, adaptability, and digital literacy. Coding, data analysis, and AI literacy are becoming essential competencies, yet access to these learning opportunities remains uneven. South Africa's education system, with its historical inequalities and challenges, faces a critical task: preparing the workforce for an unpredictable future. Without adequate investment in education and training, many workers could find themselves excluded from the job market altogether.

Despite these challenges, there are opportunities for South Africa to leverage the Fourth Industrial Revolution for growth and development. If managed well, automation and AI can unlock productivity and spur innovation across sectors. Start-ups are already embracing these technologies to solve local problems, such as using drones to deliver medical supplies to remote areas or developing AI software to enhance agricultural productivity. Additionally, South Africa's young population can be a valuable asset—if equipped with the right skills and opportunities. Policymakers, business leaders, and civil society must work together to ensure that technological change benefits everyone, not just a privileged few.

The Fourth Industrial Revolution offers a glimpse into the future—a world where machines augment human capabilities and create new possibilities. But it also challenges us to rethink the value of work and the role of humans in an increasingly automated world. Will technology liberate us from drudgery, allowing more time for creativity, community, and leisure? Or will it deepen economic divides, rendering human labour redundant and stripping millions of their sense of purpose? South Africa, like the rest of the world, stands at a crossroads. How we respond to these challenges will shape not only the future of work but also the future of human identity itself.

This chapter sets the stage for a deeper exploration of the impact of automation on society, identity, and wellbeing. As we navigate this period of profound change, we must ask difficult questions about what it means to be human in a world where machines can do much of what we once thought only people could do. The chapters that follow will delve into the human cost of automation and explore strategies for creating a future where technology serves humanity, not the other way around.

# 2 Job displacement: Sectors most vulnerable to automation

As automation continues to reshape the modern economy, one of its most pressing impacts will be the displacement of workers across various sectors. The integration of artificial intelligence (AI), robotics, and automated systems is no longer a distant possibility—it is happening now, with far-reaching consequences. The shift towards automation promises greater efficiency, precision, and cost savings, but it also presents significant challenges, especially for those whose livelihoods are built on tasks that machines are increasingly capable of performing. In South Africa, this phenomenon is not just a theoretical concern. The reality of job displacement is becoming evident in industries that have traditionally been the backbone of employment in both urban and rural areas. As technology advances, certain sectors are more vulnerable to automation than others, and understanding where these vulnerabilities lie is essential to prepare for the challenges ahead.

The manufacturing industry has long been the first to experience the transformative effects of automation, both globally and locally. In South Africa, the automotive sector, for instance, has integrated robotics into its production lines to streamline processes and improve efficiency. Machines are now capable of performing tasks such as welding, assembling, and quality inspection at a speed and accuracy that outpaces human labour. While these advancements increase productivity, they also reduce the need for human workers on the factory floor. Jobs that were once plentiful—such as assemblers, machine operators, and quality controllers—are gradually becoming redundant, leaving workers with limited alternatives. For communities that rely on manufacturing plants for employment, the impact of automation could deepen poverty and social inequality.

The mining industry, another cornerstone of South Africa's economy, is also facing significant disruption due to automation. With a long history of labour-intensive operations, mining companies are now turning to automated machinery to improve safety and reduce operational costs. Autonomous drilling machines, robotic loaders, and AI-based monitoring systems are replacing human workers, especially in dangerous underground environments. While automation in mining enhances safety by reducing the exposure of workers to hazardous conditions, it also means fewer jobs in a sector that has traditionally employed thousands of people, particularly in rural areas. In mining towns across the country, the decline in employment opportunities is already being felt, leading to economic instability and a rise in social challenges such as crime and substance abuse.

The retail sector is another area experiencing the disruptive effects of automation. The rise of self-checkout systems, automated inventory management, and AI-powered customer service bots is reducing the need for cashiers, stock controllers, and shop assistants. In urban centres such as Johannesburg and Cape Town, large retail chains are already adopting these technologies to streamline operations and cut costs. While automation allows for faster service and improved customer experience, it also displaces workers, particularly those in entry-level positions. For many young people entering the job market for the first time, retail jobs have traditionally provided a foothold into the world of work. With these opportunities now shrinking, young job seekers are left with fewer options, exacerbating the already high youth unemployment rate.

The transport and logistics sector, which plays a crucial role in moving goods across the country, is also undergoing significant changes due to automation. Driverless vehicles, autonomous drones, and AI-based logistics systems are being tested and implemented to enhance efficiency and reduce costs. South African transport companies are beginning to explore the use of automated trucks for long-haul routes, which, if widely adopted, could have a substantial impact on the livelihoods of truck drivers. Similarly, the use of drones for deliveries—particularly in rural and remote areas—has the potential to replace human delivery workers. While these innovations improve logistical efficiency, they also pose a risk to the job security of thousands of workers who rely on driving, delivery, and freight jobs for their income.

The financial sector, traditionally seen as a space for human expertise and decision-making, is not immune to automation either. AI algorithms and robotic process automation (RPA) are increasingly being used to perform tasks such as data analysis, fraud detection, and customer service. Chatbots are replacing call centre agents, and automated systems are handling loan applications and credit assessments. In cities like Johannesburg, which serves as a financial hub for the region, many jobs in banking and insurance are becoming susceptible to automation. Administrative roles and entry-level positions, which previously offered stable employment, are being replaced by software solutions. While these technologies improve service efficiency, they also create uncertainty for employees, especially those without specialised skills to transition into new roles.

The agricultural sector, although traditionally labour-intensive, is also seeing the effects of automation. Technologies such as precision farming, automated tractors, and AI-driven crop monitoring systems are gradually being introduced to enhance productivity. These innovations allow farmers to manage larger areas of land with fewer workers, reducing the need for manual labour in planting, harvesting, and irrigation. In rural areas of South

Africa, where farming provides vital employment, the adoption of automation presents a difficult trade-off between increased agricultural efficiency and the displacement of workers. Farmworkers, who often lack access to re-skilling opportunities, face significant challenges in finding alternative employment in a rapidly changing economy.

The hospitality sector, particularly hotels and restaurants, is not immune to the wave of automation either. Service robots are being introduced in hotels to handle tasks such as cleaning and room service, while automated ordering systems are becoming common in fast-food restaurants. Although the hospitality industry remains dependent on human interaction to a degree, especially in customer-facing roles, the adoption of automation is reducing the need for back-of-house staff. For South Africa's tourism industry, which plays a vital role in the economy, these changes could alter the employment landscape, particularly in cities like Cape Town and Durban, where tourism is a major source of jobs.

As automation continues to advance, the sectors most vulnerable to job displacement reflect the complex interplay between technology and the labour market. While automation brings undeniable benefits, such as improved efficiency, cost savings, and safety, it also presents significant challenges. For many workers, the loss of a job is not just a financial blow—it represents a loss of purpose, identity, and community connection. In a country like South Africa, where unemployment is already a critical issue, the displacement of workers due to automation could exacerbate social inequality and deepen the divide between those with access to digital skills and those without.

The challenge lies in how South Africa navigates this transition. As jobs in traditional sectors become scarcer, there is an urgent need to invest in education and re-skilling programmes to prepare workers for new opportunities in the digital economy. Policymakers must work with businesses to ensure that the benefits of automation are shared equitably, and that those most affected by job displacement are not left behind. Innovation and entrepreneurship will play a key role in creating new forms of work, but these efforts must be supported by policies that promote inclusivity and social protection.

The displacement of jobs by automation is not just a South African issue—it is a global challenge. However, the unique socio-economic context of South Africa requires tailored solutions that consider the country's historical inequalities and current realities. As the following chapters will explore, addressing the human cost of automation requires a collective effort from government, businesses, communities, and individuals. By understanding which sectors are most vulnerable and taking proactive steps to mitigate the impact, South Africa can navigate the challenges of automation and build a future where technology enhances, rather than erodes, human dignity.

# 3 The pace of change: Accelerating technological advancements

The speed at which technology is advancing today is unprecedented. In the past, transformative innovations such as the printing press, steam engine, or electricity took decades—if not centuries—to fully reshape societies. But in the 21st century, change is happening almost overnight, with new technologies constantly being developed, tested, and integrated into everyday life. From artificial intelligence (AI) to blockchain, robotics, and quantum computing, the rapid pace of change is leaving businesses, governments, and individuals scrambling to keep up. While this accelerating innovation promises significant benefits, it also brings immense challenges—especially for those whose livelihoods depend on more traditional ways of working. South Africa, like much of the world, is standing on the edge of this technological revolution, and the rapid pace of change is already disrupting industries and communities at a rate many are struggling to comprehend.

One of the defining characteristics of this era is the exponential nature of technological growth. Unlike the gradual progress of previous revolutions, today's advancements build on one another at breakneck speed. For example, artificial intelligence systems, once the stuff of science fiction, are now evolving at such a rapid pace that their capabilities double every few years. Machine learning algorithms that initially required months to process data are now improving themselves in real-time, rendering older systems obsolete within months. In South Africa's financial sector, for instance, AI-powered chatbots and virtual assistants have quickly replaced human customer service agents, reducing costs for businesses but creating uncertainty for workers. The same trend can be seen in industries ranging from retail to healthcare, where AI is driving innovations faster than policies or job markets can adapt.

The pace of change is also being accelerated by the convergence of multiple technologies. Developments in one field often spur advances in others, creating a domino effect of innovation. Robotics, for example, is not evolving in isolation—it is being combined with AI, cloud computing, and the Internet of Things (IoT) to produce autonomous systems that can learn, adapt, and operate independently. In South Africa, automated warehouses are already becoming a reality, with robots handling stock management and logistics more efficiently than human workers ever could. Similarly, the transport sector is on the brink of disruption, with the testing of autonomous vehicles and drones set to transform the way goods and people move across the country. While these innovations promise efficiency and lower costs, they raise complex questions about what role human labour will play in this increasingly automated landscape.

The shift towards automation is further accelerated by the global nature of technological development. Advances in one part of the world are quickly adopted elsewhere, creating a ripple effect that amplifies the rate of change. South Africa is not immune to these global trends. The country is already importing cutting-edge technologies from markets like China, the United States, and Europe, integrating them into local industries and supply chains. However, the rapid adoption of these technologies can also expose the country's vulnerabilities. With limited time to adapt, businesses, workers, and policymakers often find themselves reacting to change rather than proactively shaping it. The result is a growing skills gap, as many workers are unable to keep pace with the demands of new technologies, leaving them vulnerable to job displacement.

One of the most significant challenges posed by the rapid pace of technological advancement is the shortening of industry lifecycles. In the past, workers could expect to stay in the same profession or industry for most of their careers, gradually mastering their skills over time. Today, however, entire industries are being disrupted within a matter of years. Technologies that were considered state-of-the-art just a few years ago can quickly become outdated, replaced by newer, more efficient solutions. Workers in sectors like IT and manufacturing, where constant technological upgrades are the norm, are under increasing pressure to continuously upskill just to remain employable. In South Africa, this dynamic is particularly challenging, as access to quality education and training opportunities remains uneven, exacerbating the digital divide between those with the skills to thrive in the new economy and those left behind.

The pace of change also presents challenges for policymakers, who must grapple with the need to regulate emerging technologies while fostering innovation. Governments are often slow to react to rapid technological shifts, creating a lag between the development of new technologies and the establishment of policies to govern their use. This lag can lead to significant risks, such as the misuse of AI systems or the rise of unregulated gig work platforms, which exploit workers in the absence of proper labour protections. In South Africa, the gig economy— enabled by apps and platforms—has grown rapidly, providing short-term employment opportunities but also contributing to job insecurity. The challenge for policymakers is to strike a balance between enabling innovation and ensuring that the benefits of technological progress are shared equitably across society.

At the heart of the accelerating pace of technological change is the tension between opportunity and disruption. On the one hand, new technologies offer incredible potential to solve some of society's most pressing challenges. AI-powered healthcare solutions, for instance, can improve diagnostic accuracy and make medical care more accessible, particularly in rural areas. Automation in agriculture can increase food production and reduce waste, helping to address food insecurity. However, these benefits come with significant trade-offs. As machines become more capable of performing tasks traditionally done by humans, the question of what role people will play in the economy becomes more urgent. In a country like South Africa, where unemployment is already high, the displacement of workers by technology could deepen social inequalities and create new challenges for social cohesion.

While the rapid pace of technological change is often viewed as inevitable, it is not beyond human control. The choices made today—by governments, businesses, and individuals—will shape how this transition unfolds. Investing in education and re-skilling programmes is essential to prepare workers for the jobs of the future, but it is equally important to foster a culture of lifelong learning that enables people to adapt to continuous change. Businesses must recognise their responsibility to manage the impact of automation on their workforce, providing support for displaced workers and creating opportunities for retraining. Policymakers must be proactive in shaping a regulatory framework that encourages innovation while safeguarding workers' rights and ensuring that no one is left behind.

Ultimately, the challenge posed by the accelerating

pace of technological advancement is not just about managing change—it is about reimagining the future of work and redefining what it means to contribute to society. If handled thoughtfully, the transition to an automated economy can create opportunities for meaningful work that goes beyond traditional employment. By embracing new technologies in ways that complement human capabilities, rather than replacing them, South Africa can build a future where technology enhances the quality of life for all its citizens. However, achieving this vision will require a collective effort, guided by a commitment to inclusivity, fairness, and social justice. As the pace of change continues to accelerate, the choices we make today will determine whether automation becomes a force for empowerment or a source of division. The future is uncertain, but it is also within our power to shape.

# 4 Global implications: The worldwide impact of automation

Automation is not just a local or national phenomenon; it is a wave that is sweeping across the globe, reshaping economies, industries, and societies in profound ways. From Silicon Valley to Shenzhen, automation is driving a new world order where machines and algorithms are becoming central to how things are produced, managed, and delivered. The implications are vast and complex—creating new opportunities while threatening existing livelihoods. The world is becoming increasingly interconnected, and automation's ripple effects are being felt everywhere, from developed nations with advanced economies to developing countries like South Africa, where technology presents both promise and peril. Understanding the global scope of automation helps frame the challenges we face locally within a broader context, highlighting the need for coordinated strategies that balance progress with inclusivity.

In developed countries, automation has taken hold across many sectors, especially those reliant on repetitive, process-driven work. Advanced economies like Germany, Japan, and the United States have already integrated robotics into manufacturing, significantly increasing productivity while reducing reliance on human labour. This has enabled them to lower production costs and remain competitive in global markets, but it has also led to the shrinking of traditional blue-collar jobs that once sustained working-class families. In countries like the United States, the shift towards automation has accelerated the decline of industries such as steel production, coal mining, and car manufacturing—industries that were once the backbone of entire communities. As machines take over jobs, these regions are grappling with rising unemployment, inequality, and social unrest, raising difficult questions about how to provide displaced workers with new economic opportunities.

In the Global South, automation presents a different but equally complex set of challenges. For many developing nations, manufacturing and labour-intensive industries have historically provided a pathway out of poverty. However, automation is disrupting this trajectory. Countries that once relied on low-cost labour to attract foreign investment—such as Bangladesh, Indonesia, and even South Africa—are facing the harsh reality that machines can now perform tasks more efficiently than human workers. Automation threatens to displace jobs in sectors like textiles, agriculture, and mining, industries that employ millions and form the economic backbone of many African countries. If companies can produce goods more cheaply using machines in their home countries, the competitive advantage of outsourcing to regions with lower labour costs begins to disappear. This shift could lead to significant job losses in Africa and deepen economic inequality between developed and developing nations.

At the same time, automation is reshaping the nature of work in ways that are creating new forms of inequality. The rise of gig platforms, remote work technologies, and freelance opportunities is enabling some workers to participate in the global economy, but these benefits are not distributed evenly. In wealthier countries, workers with access to high-speed internet and digital skills are thriving, while those without these resources are being left behind. The digital divide is becoming a critical issue, as countries without the infrastructure or educational systems to prepare their populations for the digital economy risk falling further behind. In South Africa, for example, access to technology and skills remains uneven, with rural areas and disadvantaged communities struggling to keep up with the demands of the automated future. This global divide in access to technology is reinforcing existing patterns of inequality, creating a new class of "digital haves" and "have-nots."

Another significant global implication of automation is the potential for economic instability. As machines become more efficient and capable, companies are likely to rely less on human labour, leading to job losses that could weaken consumer spending. This is particularly concerning for economies that are heavily dependent on consumer demand, as fewer employed people mean less disposable income circulating in the economy. Some economists warn that automation could trigger a "deflationary spiral," where falling demand leads to lower prices and profits, prompting businesses to cut costs further by automating even more jobs. This cycle could create long-term economic stagnation, especially in regions that do not develop policies to support displaced workers or promote new industries. South Africa's high unemployment rate makes it particularly vulnerable to these dynamics, as automation could exacerbate the job crisis unless proactive measures are taken.

The environmental impact of automation is also a growing concern. On the one hand, automation holds the potential to reduce waste, improve energy efficiency, and make production processes more sustainable. For instance, AI-driven systems can optimise supply chains, ensuring that resources are used more effectively and reducing carbon footprints. Automated agriculture could help address food insecurity by increasing crop yields and reducing water usage. However, these benefits come with environmental trade-offs. The production of robots, AI systems, and other automated technologies requires significant amounts of rare minerals and energy, contributing to environmental degradation and climate change. Furthermore, the disposal of obsolete machines and electronic waste presents a growing environmental challenge, particularly for countries in the Global South, which often lack the infrastructure to manage e-waste responsibly. Balancing the environmental benefits of automation with its ecological costs will require coordinated global efforts and sustainable development strategies.

The political implications of automation are also unfolding on the global stage, as governments grapple with how to regulate emerging technologies while addressing the social and economic disruptions they create. In some countries, the rise of automation is contributing to growing populism and political polarisation, as workers who feel left behind by technological change express their frustration at the ballot box. The fear of job loss and economic insecurity has fuelled anti-globalisation movements, with some governments adopting protectionist policies in an attempt to shield their industries from automation's impact. South Africa is not immune to these dynamics, as political pressure to address unemployment and inequality intensifies. Policymakers must navigate a delicate balancing act— embracing automation to remain competitive while ensuring that the social fabric is not torn apart by rising inequality and job displacement.

At the same time, the global nature of automation requires international cooperation. No single country can manage the challenges of automation in isolation, as technological advancements transcend borders and affect economies worldwide. Countries must collaborate to develop frameworks for managing the ethical and social implications of automation, ensuring that its benefits are shared equitably. Discussions around Universal Basic Income (UBI), international labour standards, and cross-border taxation are already taking place, as governments explore ways to cushion the impact of automation on workers and ensure that multinational corporations contribute their fair share to the societies they operate in. South Africa has an opportunity to participate in these global conversations, shaping policies that reflect the unique challenges and aspirations of developing nations.

Ultimately, the global implications of automation highlight the need for a new social contract—one that recognises the transformative power of technology while prioritising human dignity and well-being. Automation is reshaping economies and societies at an unprecedented pace, but it does not have to lead to a future of inequality and exclusion. By investing in education, re-skilling programmes, and social safety nets, countries can empower their citizens to adapt to the changing world of work. Businesses must also play their part by adopting responsible automation strategies that balance efficiency with fairness. And governments must take the lead in crafting policies that promote innovation while safeguarding the rights and livelihoods of their people.

The global impact of automation is both a challenge and an opportunity. While it threatens to disrupt traditional ways of working, it also offers the chance to reimagine what work can be—creating a future where technology enhances human potential rather than replacing it. For South Africa, the road ahead will not be easy, but it is also full of possibility. By learning from the experiences of other countries and embracing a collaborative approach, we can shape a future where automation serves as a force for progress, inclusion, and shared prosperity. The challenge is daunting, but the opportunity to create a more just and sustainable world is within our reach.

# Part 2: The Human Cost

# THE END OF WORK

# 5 Identity crisis: The psychological impact of job loss

Work has always been more than just a way to earn a living—it shapes who we are, how we see ourselves, and how we engage with the world around us. For many people, their job is closely tied to their identity, giving them a sense of purpose, structure, and belonging. Whether it's a miner in Mpumalanga, a teacher in Cape Town, or a factory worker in Gauteng, having a job often provides individuals with more than financial security; it offers a reason to get up in the morning, a way to contribute to society, and a sense of personal worth. However, the rise of automation is threatening to upend this connection between work and identity, creating an identity crisis that runs deeper than unemployment alone. When people lose their jobs to machines or algorithms, it isn't just the loss of income that hurts—it is the loss of meaning, status, and a place in the social fabric.

The psychological impact of job loss can be devastating, as many displaced workers find themselves questioning their value in society. For decades, society has conditioned people to believe that their worth is tied to their productivity. The idea that hard work is the path to success is ingrained in our culture, influencing how individuals perceive themselves and others. But what happens when even the most diligent workers are replaced by machines? Automation challenges the traditional notion that effort leads to reward, leaving workers with a profound sense of inadequacy and disorientation. For some, the loss of work can feel like the erasure of their identity. A person who once took pride in their craft—whether it was building, teaching, driving, or managing—may struggle to find a new sense of self outside the framework of employment.

In South Africa, where joblessness is already a harsh reality for many, the psychological toll of losing work to automation is likely to be even more severe. The country's high unemployment rate, particularly among the youth, has already created a generation of people struggling with feelings of failure and hopelessness. Automation threatens to intensify this crisis by displacing workers not only in traditional industries like mining and agriculture but also in service sectors such as retail, banking, and transport. A worker who is replaced by an automated teller machine or a driverless vehicle may feel discarded, as if they no longer have a role to play in society. This sense of exclusion can be deeply damaging to mental health, leading to depression, anxiety, and even social withdrawal. In communities where work is closely tied to status and dignity, the stigma of job loss can create feelings of shame and isolation, making it even harder for individuals to seek help or rebuild their lives.

The erosion of work also affects how individuals relate to their communities and families. Many people derive a sense of belonging and social identity from their workplaces, forming relationships and networks that shape their lives beyond the job itself. When a worker is displaced, these connections can be disrupted, leaving them feeling alienated from their social circles. This is particularly true for men, who, in many cultures, are still expected to be breadwinners and providers. In South Africa, where traditional gender roles remain influential, the loss of work can challenge a man's sense of masculinity, leading to emotional turmoil and strained family relationships. Without the structure and purpose that work provides, individuals may struggle to maintain routines, leading to a loss of motivation and a breakdown in personal relationships. Marriages can come under strain, and children may feel the emotional fallout of parents grappling with a sense of failure.

The psychological effects of job loss are not limited to individuals—they ripple through communities as well. In places where industries have declined, the loss of work can lead to a breakdown of social cohesion, with entire neighbourhoods experiencing the effects of poverty, crime, and disillusionment. Towns built around industries—such as mining communities in the Northern Cape or manufacturing hubs in KwaZulu-Natal—can become ghost towns when automation renders these jobs obsolete. The collective identity of such communities, often tied to shared labour, can crumble, leading to increased social unrest. A sense of hopelessness can take root, fuelling substance abuse, violence, and other social problems.

The mental health consequences of job loss to automation require urgent attention, but the challenge lies in addressing a problem that is deeply tied to societal expectations about work. Many people find it difficult to seek help for mental health struggles, especially in cultures where vulnerability is seen as weakness. In South Africa, mental health services are often under-resourced, making it difficult for displaced workers to access the support they need. The stigma surrounding mental illness further complicates matters, leaving many people to suffer in silence. Without meaningful interventions, the psychological fallout of automation could become a silent epidemic, undermining the well-being of individuals, families, and entire communities.

Rebuilding a sense of identity in a world where traditional work is becoming less central will require a shift in how society defines value and purpose. People need to be encouraged to see themselves as more than their jobs, finding meaning in activities, relationships, and contributions that extend beyond the workplace. This might involve reimagining education systems to emphasise personal growth and social engagement rather than simply preparing individuals for the labour market. It also means creating spaces for people to connect, collaborate, and contribute to their communities in ways that do not rely solely on paid employment. Volunteer work, creative pursuits, and community projects can provide alternative avenues for purpose, helping people reclaim their sense of worth outside the framework of traditional jobs.

Policymakers, businesses, and mental health professionals all have a role to play in supporting individuals through this transition. Governments need to invest in mental health services and social safety nets that address not only financial insecurity but also the emotional impact of job loss. Businesses should prioritise responsible automation strategies, offering retraining programmes and mental health support for displaced workers. Community organisations can play a vital role in fostering resilience, creating opportunities for social connection and personal growth. South Africa's history of overcoming adversity through collective action offers valuable lessons in building solidarity and hope during times of change.

Ultimately, the identity crisis triggered by automation forces us to confront fundamental questions about what it means to be human in a world where machines can perform many of the tasks that once defined us. While the challenges are significant, they also present an opportunity to rethink how we define success, value, and purpose. By fostering a culture that values people for who they are, rather than what they do, we can begin to build a society where identity is no longer tethered to employment alone. The road ahead will not be easy, but it is also a chance to create a future where every individual's worth is recognised, regardless of whether they hold a job or not. If we can embrace this shift, we may discover new ways of living, working, and thriving in the age of automation.

# 6 Social disintegration: Community and family structures under threat

Work has long been a binding force in communities, providing structure, stability, and connection. In South Africa, jobs have often served as lifelines not only for individuals but also for families and neighbourhoods, ensuring the social fabric remains intact. The factory worker in Durban, the teacher in Soweto, or the miner in Rustenburg—beyond earning wages, their labour has given them a role in their families and local communities. However, as automation increasingly replaces human effort, the impact will go far beyond the loss of income. The erosion of work threatens to weaken the social glue that holds families and communities together, resulting in deep fractures in both personal relationships and communal bonds. With work being a central part of our daily lives, its absence could destabilise the very structures that foster collective identity, belonging, and support.

For many South Africans, employment provides more than just financial security—it shapes routines and rhythms within families. Having predictable work hours gives structure to households: parents who leave in the morning and return in the evening create a routine around which meals, schoolwork, and other activities are organised. When that structure is lost, families often experience a breakdown in discipline, communication, and connection. As automation displaces more people from the workforce, traditional routines that have provided predictability and stability may begin to unravel. Without the structure of work, some individuals may fall into unhealthy habits, such as idleness, substance abuse, or chronic disengagement from family responsibilities. Children, in particular, are vulnerable to the consequences of these disruptions, as they are heavily dependent on consistent parental involvement to thrive.

The absence of work can also strain relationships within households. In many South African homes, particularly those still shaped by traditional gender roles, the male breadwinner carries the responsibility of providing for the family. When that role is disrupted by job loss, it can trigger feelings of inadequacy and frustration. Men, in particular, may struggle to adjust to a new reality in which they no longer fulfil the role of provider. This frustration can manifest as withdrawal from family life or, in some cases, result in conflict and tension within the household. In other cases, women may take on greater financial burdens by joining the workforce or engaging in informal economic activities, which can shift family dynamics and place new pressures on relationships. When these changes occur abruptly due to job loss, families may find it difficult to adapt, leading to arguments, resentment, and emotional distance between partners.

In South African communities where work has

traditionally provided a sense of belonging and identity, job loss threatens to fracture social cohesion. In places like the mining towns of Mpumalanga or agricultural hubs in the Western Cape, the loss of jobs to automation can leave communities adrift. Historically, shared employment experiences— whether in factories, on farms, or in mines—have fostered a sense of solidarity and mutual support among workers. These bonds often extend beyond the workplace, shaping how individuals connect through sports clubs, stokvels (community savings groups), or religious organisations. When jobs disappear, these networks begin to weaken. A community that once found pride in its shared labour may face an identity crisis, leaving residents feeling disconnected from each other. The loss of collective purpose can fuel feelings of isolation and hopelessness, making it harder for people to come together and tackle common challenges.

The weakening of community structures caused by automation also leaves space for social problems to take root. In areas where joblessness becomes widespread, crime rates tend to increase as people turn to desperate measures to survive. Substance abuse, already a significant issue in many South African communities, often escalates when individuals lose hope and access to meaningful activities. With fewer job opportunities, young people in particular are at risk of disengaging from both education and community life, creating a generation that feels alienated and disconnected from society. Schools, churches, and community organisations—while valuable—may struggle to fill the void left by the loss of employment opportunities, especially in under-resourced areas.

The loss of work can also have far-reaching implications for intergenerational relationships. In many South African families, children grow up observing their parents or caregivers working hard to provide for them, learning values like discipline, perseverance, and responsibility in the process. When work disappears, these lessons may no longer be as visible or relevant, making it harder for young people to develop a sense of purpose and direction. Young people who see their parents struggling with unemployment may lose faith in the idea that hard work leads to success, resulting in a generational cycle of disengagement from work and education. As traditional pathways to stability and progress become less accessible, families may struggle to pass on hope and ambition to the next generation.

Another challenge lies in the erosion of informal community safety nets, which have traditionally provided support to vulnerable members of society. In South African townships and rural areas, people often rely on extended family networks and neighbours for help in times of need. When automation displaces workers, it reduces the financial capacity of individuals to participate in these mutual support systems, leaving vulnerable members of society—such as the elderly, children, and people with disabilities—without sufficient care. As more households face financial instability, the burden of supporting relatives and neighbours becomes heavier, stretching the capacity of communities to care for one another. The weakening of these safety nets makes it more difficult to address collective challenges, such as poverty and inequality.

Addressing the social disintegration caused by job loss will require more than just economic interventions—it demands a reimagining of community life and family structures. To rebuild and strengthen communities, policymakers must recognise the importance of meaningful social activities that foster belonging and solidarity. Initiatives that promote community involvement—such as sports programmes, cultural activities, and volunteer opportunities—can help people reconnect with one another, providing new ways to build identity and purpose outside of formal employment. Support for community-led initiatives will also be crucial in filling the gaps left by disappearing jobs, offering people opportunities to participate in meaningful projects that improve their local environments.

At the same time, families will need to find new ways to adapt to a future where work is no longer the defining feature of daily life. Open communication, emotional support, and shared activities can help families maintain connection and resilience during periods of uncertainty. Men and women alike will need to renegotiate family roles in ways that reflect the realities of automation, fostering partnerships that are based on shared responsibilities rather than traditional gender expectations.

The role of government, business, and civil society in supporting these transitions cannot be overstated. Policies that promote job creation, education, and mental health services will be essential to easing the impact of automation on communities and families. Businesses, too, have a responsibility to engage with communities, offering retraining programmes and ensuring that the benefits of technological advancement are shared widely. Community organisations can play a vital role in fostering resilience and social cohesion by creating spaces for people to connect, share, and grow together.

Ultimately, automation need not lead to the collapse of social structures—if we can find new ways to connect, support, and care for one another, it may offer an opportunity to rebuild communities on foundations of compassion and cooperation. While the challenges are significant, they are also an invitation to reimagine how we live and work together. By fostering a culture that values relationships and community as much as productivity, South Africans can build a future where families and neighbourhoods remain strong, even as the nature of work changes. In navigating the disruptions of automation, we have the chance to create a society that places human connection at its core—a future where people are valued not for what they produce, but for who they are and the communities they help build.

# 7 Mental health concerns: Anxiety, depression, and isolation

The loss of employment doesn't just impact one's financial situation; it takes a profound toll on mental health. In South Africa, where work is often closely tied to dignity, identity, and social standing, job loss or the fear of becoming redundant can lead to severe emotional strain. Automation introduces an unsettling level of uncertainty, as people see jobs around them slowly replaced by machines, algorithms, and AI systems. The threat of irrelevance can trigger deep-seated anxiety, depression, and a growing sense of isolation among workers who struggle to adapt to this shifting reality. This psychological impact is not limited to those who have already lost their jobs—it ripples through society, creating fear and insecurity even among those still employed.

At its core, work provides more than just a source of income. It is often a means of self-expression and purpose. For many South Africans, having a job signifies that they are contributing to society and providing for their families. The workplace becomes a space where individuals forge relationships, build self-esteem, and experience a sense of belonging. When this connection to work is severed or when the prospect of job loss looms large, the absence of purpose can feel overwhelming. People may begin to question their worth, leading to a crisis of identity that can quickly spiral into anxiety and depression. Many individuals describe the experience of unemployment as feeling as though the ground has shifted beneath their feet, leaving them unmoored from any sense of stability or future direction.

The stress brought on by automation is particularly acute for workers in vulnerable sectors, such as manufacturing, retail, and transport, where machines and AI are rapidly replacing human labour. Workers who lack advanced technical skills often find themselves trapped in cycles of uncertainty, unable to secure new employment or acquire the necessary training to remain relevant in the job market. This uncertainty creates a constant undercurrent of anxiety, as people wonder when or if they, too, will be replaced. The resulting mental strain can have devastating consequences, with individuals experiencing panic attacks, sleeplessness, and chronic stress. Over time, the burden of living under this pressure can erode emotional resilience, leaving people susceptible to long-term mental health conditions.

Depression, too, is a common outcome of job loss, especially when individuals find it difficult to re-enter the workforce. In South Africa, the stigma associated with unemployment can compound feelings of shame and hopelessness, making it harder for individuals to seek help. Men, in particular, often bear the emotional brunt of job loss, as societal expectations still place significant value on their ability to provide. When they are no longer able to meet these expectations, many withdraw emotionally, internalising their struggles. This can lead to a cycle of depression, where the loss of work not only damages their sense of self but also undermines their ability to actively seek new opportunities. Overwhelmed by the sense of failure, some individuals may disengage from family life and social interactions altogether, further deepening their isolation.

The isolation that accompanies unemployment is another significant mental health concern. Workplaces are not just spaces of productivity—they are social environments where people build friendships and networks of support. Without the daily interactions that come with having a job, many individuals find themselves disconnected from these essential social connections. This isolation can become especially acute in rural areas and townships, where limited access to social activities and community engagement exacerbates feelings of loneliness. For some, the shame of joblessness prevents them from participating in community life or reaching out for help, creating a sense of invisibility. As social isolation deepens, it becomes increasingly difficult for individuals to regain the motivation and energy needed to reconnect with society or rebuild their lives.

The mental health crisis linked to automation is not just an individual problem—it is a societal challenge. Families, too, bear the emotional fallout of job loss.

Children growing up in households affected by unemployment are more likely to experience emotional distress, especially if they witness their parents struggling with anxiety and depression. The stress of financial insecurity can strain relationships between spouses and parents, leading to conflict and emotional distance within the household. Over time, these tensions can fracture family bonds, creating an environment where emotional support becomes scarce. In communities where unemployment is widespread, these personal struggles accumulate, contributing to a collective sense of despair and hopelessness.

The absence of accessible mental health services compounds these challenges. In South Africa, mental health care is often underfunded and difficult to access, particularly in rural areas and townships. Many people suffering from anxiety or depression are reluctant to seek help due to stigma or a lack of awareness about available resources. Even when individuals do reach out, they may encounter long waiting times, a shortage of qualified professionals, or unaffordable treatment options. For those experiencing job loss and financial strain, these barriers can feel insurmountable. As a result, many people suffer in silence, their mental health deteriorating without intervention or support.

However, addressing the mental health impact of automation requires more than just clinical solutions—it demands a broader reimagining of how society values people beyond their economic contributions. Policymakers, businesses, and communities must work together to build environments that prioritise mental well-being and offer support during periods of transition. This includes expanding access to counselling and mental health services, particularly in vulnerable communities where job loss is most likely to occur. Employers, too, have a role to play by offering support programmes for workers facing redundancy and promoting mental health awareness in the workplace.

In addition to formal interventions, community-based initiatives can provide essential support for individuals dealing with anxiety, depression, and isolation. Support groups, mentorship programmes, and community projects can create opportunities for people to connect, share their experiences, and rebuild their sense of purpose. Churches, sports clubs, and cultural organisations also have an important role in fostering social connection and providing emotional support. By creating spaces where people feel seen and valued, communities can help individuals navigate the emotional challenges of job loss and rebuild their lives.

Ultimately, the mental health challenges posed by automation highlight the need for a more compassionate society—one that recognises that people are more than their productivity. As we navigate the transition to an automated future, we must ensure that mental well-being is prioritised alongside economic adaptation. South Africa has a long history of resilience in the face of adversity, and this moment is no different. By fostering a culture of care, connection, and mental health awareness, we can help individuals and communities navigate the emotional challenges of a changing world and emerge stronger on the other side. The future of work may be uncertain, but the value of human connection and well-being is timeless.

# 8 Economic insecurity: The erosion of financial stability

Economic insecurity is one of the most tangible and devastating consequences of automation, especially in South Africa, where unemployment and inequality are already pressing issues. The gradual replacement of human workers with machines and artificial intelligence threatens to erode the financial stability of individuals, families, and entire communities. Automation not only eliminates jobs but also creates a sense of unpredictability, making it difficult for workers to plan for the future. When employment opportunities shrink, the financial foundations upon which people build their lives—buying homes, educating children, or even meeting basic daily needs—begin to crumble.

In South Africa, many households operate on razor-thin financial margins, with large portions of the population living paycheque to paycheque. When jobs are lost due to automation, the loss of income often means an immediate descent into economic hardship. Breadwinners who once supported extended families find themselves unable to meet their obligations, forcing households to make painful choices between essentials like food, school fees, and healthcare. As the stress of financial insecurity sets in, it begins to ripple through all areas of life, placing enormous pressure on personal relationships and mental well-being. The emotional weight of knowing that one's livelihood could vanish overnight takes a toll not only on workers but on entire families.

Automation further exacerbates existing inequalities, creating a divide between those who can adapt to the changing economy and those left behind. Workers with higher levels of education and specialised skills may find new opportunities in emerging industries, but many others, especially those in manual labour or repetitive jobs, face a bleaker reality. South Africa's education system and job market are already struggling with a mismatch between skills and employment opportunities. As automation advances, the gap between the "employable" and the unemployed widens, leaving large segments of the population locked out of the formal economy. This growing inequality threatens to intensify poverty and deepen social divisions, particularly in communities that are already marginalised.

The decline of stable employment also undermines long-term financial planning. Traditional markers of adulthood and security—such as owning a home, saving for retirement, and building generational wealth—become increasingly unattainable in an economy where jobs are scarce or precarious. Without stable income, many South Africans are forced to rely on short-term or informal work, which often lacks benefits such as medical aid, pension contributions, or paid leave. This insecurity makes it nearly impossible for individuals to plan for the future or build a safety net for times of crisis. As a result, more people are pushed into cycles of debt, borrowing to cover basic expenses and becoming trapped in a financial spiral that is difficult to escape.

The erosion of financial stability also poses significant risks to the broader economy. South Africa relies heavily on consumer spending to drive economic growth, but when people lose their jobs or experience reduced income, their purchasing power shrinks. This decline in consumer demand can create a domino effect, with businesses forced to downsize or close, leading to further job losses and economic contraction. Small and medium-sized enterprises, which are essential to job creation in South Africa, are particularly vulnerable in this environment. Without a stable customer base, many of these businesses struggle to survive, and their collapse further exacerbates the unemployment crisis.

For young people entering the job market, the erosion of financial stability presents a daunting challenge. Many graduates emerge from university with high hopes but encounter a harsh reality—jobs are scarce, and competition is fierce. Automation reduces the availability of entry-level positions, making it harder for young people to gain work experience and establish themselves professionally. For those unable to find employment, the transition to adulthood becomes a period of prolonged economic dependence, with many forced to rely on family support well into their twenties or thirties. This delays key life milestones, such as moving out of the family home, starting a family, or building financial independence, further deepening the sense of economic stagnation.

Social grants and government assistance programmes, though critical in alleviating extreme poverty, cannot fully address the challenges of economic insecurity. While South Africa's social safety net provides temporary relief, it is not designed to replace the dignity and empowerment that come from meaningful employment. As more people find themselves unemployed or underemployed, the strain on these systems grows, and the state's ability to provide adequate support is stretched thin. This creates a dangerous dynamic in which individuals and families remain trapped in cycles of dependency, with little opportunity to break free and build sustainable livelihoods.

In the face of these challenges, some individuals turn to the informal economy as a means of survival. South Africa has a vibrant informal sector, from street vendors and taxi drivers to domestic workers and small traders. While this sector provides an essential safety net for many, it is also marked by instability and limited earnings. Workers in the informal economy are often excluded from labour protections and social benefits, leaving them vulnerable to exploitation and economic shocks. Automation may further disrupt the informal sector by introducing new technologies, such as delivery drones and ride-hailing apps, which replace traditional jobs. This could diminish the already fragile livelihoods of millions who depend on informal work to make ends meet.

Despite the daunting nature of economic insecurity, there are also opportunities to reimagine financial stability in an automated world. Policymakers, businesses, and civil society must explore new approaches to economic inclusion, such as universal basic income (UBI) and expanded access to education and skills training. UBI, for example, could provide a guaranteed financial cushion, ensuring that people have the means to survive even as jobs disappear. Similarly, targeted investment in education and vocational training can help workers transition into new roles in industries that are less vulnerable to automation. These solutions, however, require bold leadership, collaborative effort, and a willingness to rethink traditional economic models.

The private sector also has a crucial role to play in mitigating the impact of automation. Companies must balance the drive for efficiency with a commitment to social responsibility, ensuring that technological innovation does not come at the expense of human well-being. This could involve creating new kinds of jobs that complement automation rather than replace it, or investing in the upskilling and retraining of employees. Additionally, partnerships between businesses, government, and non-profit organisations can foster inclusive economic growth by supporting entrepreneurship and job creation in underserved communities.

Ultimately, addressing economic insecurity in the face of automation will require a collective effort. South Africa must confront the challenges of automation head-on, developing policies and initiatives that prioritise financial stability and economic resilience. While automation presents undeniable risks, it also offers an opportunity to build a more inclusive and equitable economy—one that recognises the value of all people, not just their productivity. As we navigate the transition to a new world of work, it is essential to ensure that no one is left behind. By working together to build systems of support and opportunity, we can create a future in which financial security is not a privilege but a right, accessible to all South Africans.

# Part 3: The Future of Work

# THE END OF WORK

# 9 Redefining work: Shifting perspectives on employment and purpose

As automation transforms industries and the traditional notion of employment crumbles, it becomes clear that we need to redefine the way we think about work. For centuries, work has not only been a means of survival but also a source of purpose, identity, and belonging. In South Africa, where the struggle for fair labour and decent jobs has been deeply intertwined with the fight for social justice, the idea of work is particularly loaded with meaning. Jobs are more than tasks performed in exchange for money; they have symbolised dignity, upward mobility, and inclusion in the formal economy. However, as machines, algorithms, and artificial intelligence increasingly perform tasks that once required human labour, it is time to reimagine the concept of work and explore new ways to derive purpose in a rapidly changing world.

Work has historically served as a key marker of identity, shaping how people view themselves and their role in society. In South Africa, this connection between work and identity runs deep. From mineworkers who toiled underground to teachers, nurses, and factory workers, people found meaning and pride in their contributions to the economy and their communities. A job was not only a means of earning a wage but also a way to participate in the broader social fabric. The transition to an automated economy, however, threatens to disrupt this connection. If the conventional idea of a "job" disappears or becomes irrelevant, how will individuals define themselves and find purpose? The answers to these questions require a shift in mind-set, not only about employment but also about the value we assign to activities outside of formal work.

As automation takes over routine tasks, it creates space for us to explore alternative forms of purpose—activities that may not fit within the traditional framework of paid employment but that nonetheless offer personal fulfilment and societal value. Volunteering, caregiving, mentorship, and creative pursuits could become more central to how people find meaning in their daily lives. In South Africa, where many communities rely on informal support networks, these activities are already crucial, yet they often go unrecognised or undervalued. For instance, the unpaid labour of women who care for children and the elderly plays an essential role in sustaining families and communities. As formal employment becomes more scarce, it will be important to recognise and celebrate these contributions as meaningful work in their own right.

This shift in perspective also demands a rethinking of productivity. In an economy driven by automation, the value of human input is no longer measured by hours worked or tasks completed. Instead, qualities like creativity, emotional intelligence, and the ability to connect with others may become more significant markers of contribution. For some, the idea of "working" without producing tangible outputs may feel unsettling at first, particularly in a society that has long equated productivity with worth. However, embracing new forms of value could free people from the pressure to constantly perform and allow them to focus on pursuits that enrich their lives and the lives of others. In this sense, redefining work is not only an economic necessity but also an opportunity to build a society that prioritises well-being, relationships, and community.

One of the most challenging aspects of this transition will be shifting away from the cultural expectation that full-time employment is the only legitimate path to success. Many South Africans grow up with the dream of securing a stable job, earning a regular income, and advancing in their careers. Parents, schools, and communities often reinforce the idea that employment is the ultimate goal, and those who struggle to find work are made to feel like failures. In a world where automation limits the availability of traditional jobs, clinging to these outdated ideals can only lead to frustration and exclusion. To move forward, society must embrace new narratives that allow for multiple ways of living a meaningful life, even outside the bounds of formal employment.

Redefining work also means expanding our understanding of economic empowerment. In an automated world, entrepreneurship, freelancing, and project-based work may become more common, offering individuals the flexibility to explore different interests and develop new skills. South Africa's vibrant informal economy already demonstrates the potential for self-employment and innovation, with street vendors, artisans, and small business owners finding creative ways to earn a living. However, these activities must be supported by policies that provide access to training, mentorship, and financial resources. Encouraging entrepreneurship, particularly among young people, will be essential in building an economy that can thrive alongside automation.

Education and lifelong learning will also play a crucial role in helping individuals adapt to the evolving world of work. Traditional education systems, designed to prepare students for specific jobs, may no longer meet the needs of an automated economy. Instead, there will be a growing emphasis on developing transferable skills—such as critical thinking, problem-solving, and collaboration—that can be applied across a range of contexts. Learning will need to become a continuous process, with individuals updating their skills throughout their lives to stay relevant. This shift will require a reimagining of how education is delivered, with greater use of online platforms, micro-credentials, and experiential learning opportunities.

While much of the discussion around automation focuses on the jobs that will be lost, it is important to recognise that new opportunities will also emerge. Roles in fields such as technology, renewable energy, healthcare, and the creative industries may grow, offering exciting prospects for those with the right skills and mind-set. However, not everyone will be able to make this transition smoothly, and it is essential to ensure that no one is left behind. Governments, businesses, and communities will need to work together to create inclusive policies that support people through periods of change. Social safety nets, such as universal basic income, may be necessary to provide security while individuals explore new paths and redefine their relationship with work.

Ultimately, the process of redefining work is about reclaiming control over how we live our lives. In a world increasingly dominated by technology, it is easy to feel powerless and overwhelmed. However, the transition to an automated economy offers an opportunity to rethink what truly matters and to build a society that values people not for what they produce but for who they are. Work, in its new forms, can become a space for creativity, connection, and purpose rather than a source of stress and exhaustion. By embracing new perspectives on employment and purpose, we can create a future where everyone has the opportunity to thrive, regardless of whether they hold a traditional job.

In South Africa, this journey will require bold leadership and a willingness to challenge deeply entrenched beliefs about work and success. It will also require empathy and understanding, recognising that the transition to a new world of work will be difficult for many. But if we approach this moment with openness and imagination, we have the chance to build a more inclusive, fulfilling, and sustainable way of life—one that reflects not just the demands of technology but the needs and aspirations of all people.

# 10 Universal Basic Income (UBI): A potential solution?

As automation continues to reshape industries and erode traditional employment opportunities, the concept of Universal Basic Income (UBI) has gained traction as a potential solution to the economic and social upheaval that comes with it. UBI proposes a bold yet simple idea: that every citizen, regardless of employment status, should receive a regular, unconditional sum of money from the government to cover their basic living expenses. This guaranteed income would ensure that everyone has access to the necessities of life—food, shelter, healthcare, and education—even in a world where stable jobs may become increasingly scarce. While the notion of providing money without strings attached may seem radical, it offers a way to address the deepening inequalities and insecurities of an automated future and could lay the foundation for a more humane society.

In South Africa, where unemployment remains one of the most pressing challenges, UBI has sparked significant debate. Automation threatens to worsen the already staggering unemployment figures, which sit uncomfortably high, especially among young people.

Many South Africans struggle to access stable jobs, relying instead on precarious informal work or social grants to get by. Introducing UBI in such a context would not only provide a lifeline to millions of vulnerable individuals but could also offer a more dignified alternative to the existing welfare system, which often stigmatises recipients and creates bureaucratic barriers to support. A basic income could help people meet their immediate needs without the constant fear of falling through the cracks, giving them the freedom to pursue other activities that bring personal and social value.

One of the most compelling arguments for UBI is its potential to foster resilience in a world where automation is displacing jobs at an unprecedented pace. As machines take over tasks that were once the backbone of entire industries—from mining and manufacturing to retail and customer service—many workers will find themselves out of work, through no fault of their own. The promise of retraining and reskilling may help some adapt, but not everyone will be able to make the leap into new industries, especially those who lack access to quality education or live in rural areas. UBI offers a safety net for those caught in the transition, ensuring that no one is left without the means to survive while economies shift and restructure around automation.

Critics, however, argue that UBI could discourage people from seeking employment, fostering a culture of dependency. This concern reflects a long-standing belief that work is the only legitimate way to earn one's place in society. Yet, research from pilot projects around the world—such as those conducted in Finland, Kenya, and Namibia—has shown that recipients of basic income do not stop working; rather, they are more likely to engage in meaningful activities, such as furthering their education, starting small businesses, or volunteering in their communities. In South Africa, UBI could unlock similar opportunities, especially for young people who are brimming with entrepreneurial ideas but lack the financial security to pursue them. With a guaranteed income, more individuals might explore creative and innovative avenues, helping to revitalise local economies and social networks.

Beyond the economic benefits, UBI also offers a way to restore dignity and mental well-being. In a society where many equate personal worth with employment status, joblessness can lead to feelings of shame, isolation, and hopelessness. South Africa's high unemployment rates have already taken a heavy toll on the mental health of individuals and families, contributing to rising levels of anxiety, depression, and substance abuse. A basic income would give people the breathing room to focus on personal growth, family, and community, rather than being consumed by the daily struggle to make ends meet. By reducing stress and anxiety, UBI could foster healthier, more stable communities, creating the social conditions needed to thrive in a changing world.

However, the practicalities of implementing UBI in South Africa remain a significant challenge. With an already strained public budget and pressing demands on healthcare, education, and infrastructure, finding the resources to fund a nationwide basic income would require careful planning and innovative approaches. Some propose financing UBI through wealth taxes, carbon taxes, or redistributing subsidies currently given to industries likely to be affected by automation. Others suggest that South Africa could use technology—such as blockchain or mobile payment systems—to efficiently distribute funds and reduce the risk of corruption. Regardless of the funding model, implementing UBI would require strong political will and a commitment to inclusivity, ensuring that every citizen, especially those on society's margins, benefits from the programme.

Another key consideration is how UBI would fit within South Africa's broader social and economic policies. Introducing basic income should not replace existing social grants or diminish efforts to provide quality education, healthcare, and housing. Instead, UBI should complement these efforts, providing a baseline of security that enables individuals to take advantage of other opportunities. It is essential that UBI be designed as part of a comprehensive strategy to address inequality, not merely as a stop-gap solution to the disruptions caused by automation. Policymakers would need to engage deeply with communities and stakeholders to ensure that the rollout of UBI reflects the diverse realities of South African society.

While UBI is not a silver bullet, it presents a valuable opportunity to rethink how we structure our society in an era of automation. The relentless pursuit of economic growth, often at the expense of people's well-being, has left many feeling excluded and alienated. A basic income offers the chance to create a new social contract, one that recognises the inherent worth of every individual, regardless of their ability to perform paid labour. In South Africa, where the legacies of apartheid and inequality still shape the present, UBI could be a step toward a more just and inclusive future—one where every person has the freedom to pursue their dreams, contribute to their community, and live with dignity.

The idea of UBI also challenges us to reconsider the purpose of work itself. If survival is no longer tied to employment, what becomes the role of work in our lives? This question invites us to explore new forms of meaning and purpose, beyond the confines of a traditional job. With UBI providing a foundation of security, people could pursue activities that align with their passions and values—whether that means starting a social enterprise, creating art, mentoring young people, or caring for the environment. By freeing individuals from the pressure to chase jobs that no longer exist, UBI opens the door to a future where work is not just a means to an end but a source of joy, fulfilment, and connection.

As we navigate the challenges of automation, UBI

offers a vision of what is possible when we prioritise human well-being over economic output. It invites us to imagine a future where no one is left behind, where every person has the resources they need to thrive, and where work is redefined as a creative and collaborative endeavour rather than a relentless pursuit of profit. Implementing UBI will not be easy, and it will require courage, experimentation, and a willingness to challenge deeply ingrained beliefs about work and worth. But if we succeed, we could create a society that is not only resilient in the face of automation but also more compassionate, equitable, and truly human.

# 11 Education and re-skilling: Preparing for an automated future

As automation sweeps across industries, the role of education and re-skilling has become more urgent than ever. In a world where many traditional jobs are rapidly disappearing, the ability to learn, unlearn, and adapt is no longer just an advantage but a necessity. For South Africa, this challenge is particularly pressing. With a youth unemployment rate among the highest in the world and an education system already grappling with deep-rooted inequalities, preparing for an automated future is not just about staying competitive in a global market—it's about survival. Without deliberate efforts to reimagine our approach to education and skills development, the gap between those equipped to thrive in a technology-driven world and those left behind will only grow wider.

The first step in addressing this challenge is to rethink how we approach education at its core. For too long, South Africa's education system has relied on outdated curricula that emphasise rote learning and memorisation over critical thinking, creativity, and problem-solving—skills that are crucial in an age where machines can perform repetitive tasks faster and more efficiently than humans. The focus needs to shift toward equipping learners with the tools they need to navigate uncertainty and complexity. This includes fostering digital literacy from an early age, ensuring that students are comfortable with technology not just as users but also as creators. Coding, data analytics, and artificial intelligence are no longer niche subjects; they need to be embedded within the curriculum to prepare young people for the realities of the modern economy.

But addressing the education gap requires more than just modernising school curricula. South Africa must also confront the stark inequalities that have long plagued its education system. Many learners, particularly in rural areas and disadvantaged communities, attend schools with limited access to resources—libraries, computers, or even qualified teachers. The digital divide threatens to widen as automation advances, with privileged students gaining the skills they need to compete while those from marginalised backgrounds are left even further behind. Bridging this gap will require targeted investment, not only in infrastructure but also in teacher training. Educators need to be empowered with the knowledge and tools to teach future-ready skills, ensuring that no child is excluded from opportunities to thrive in the new world of work.

Re-skilling also plays a critical role in ensuring that adults who have already entered the workforce can remain relevant in a changing economy. As entire industries transform, many workers will find that the skills they have honed over decades are no longer in demand. For factory workers, clerks, and call-centre agents—whose jobs are among the first to be automated—this can be a deeply unsettling reality. It is not simply a matter of learning new technical skills; it requires the courage to embrace change, often at a stage in life where the idea of starting over feels overwhelming. This is where government and industry must step in to support workers through accessible, affordable re-skilling programmes. These initiatives need to go beyond one-off training workshops, offering continuous learning pathways that align with emerging job opportunities.

South Africa has made some strides in this direction, but there is still a long way to go. The concept of lifelong learning must become more than just a buzzword; it needs to be woven into the fabric of our education and employment systems. Collaboration between the private sector, government, and educational institutions is crucial. Industries that stand to benefit from automation should take responsibility for re-skilling workers, while universities and vocational colleges must become more agile in responding to the changing needs of the job market. This might involve offering micro-credentials—short, focused courses that teach specific skills—so that individuals can upskill quickly and pivot into new roles without needing to commit to lengthy degree programmes.

Another key aspect of preparing for the future of work is fostering entrepreneurship and innovation. In a world where jobs may no longer be guaranteed, young people need to be encouraged to create their own opportunities. This requires an education system that nurtures creativity and resilience—one that allows learners to take risks, fail, and try again. Entrepreneurship is not just about starting businesses; it's about developing the mind-set to solve problems in innovative ways, whether that's within a start-up, a corporation, or a community initiative. Schools and universities must create spaces where young people can experiment with ideas and develop the entrepreneurial skills needed to adapt to an ever-changing world.

For South Africa, re-skilling also needs to address the specific realities of informal workers, who make up a significant portion of the labour force. Many people in the informal economy survive on small trades, street vending, or gig work, all of which are vulnerable to disruption by automation. Providing these workers with the tools to transition into new forms of economic activity is essential. This might involve offering digital skills training, financial literacy courses, and access to mentorship networks. It is also critical to recognise the valuable skills that many informal workers already possess—skills that can be formalised and expanded upon with the right support.

In preparing for an automated future, we must also rethink what success looks like in education. The traditional narrative that measures achievement by formal qualifications—matric results, diplomas, and degrees—no longer aligns with the realities of a rapidly evolving job market. Success in the future will be defined not only by what people know but by their ability to learn new things continuously. Soft skills such as adaptability, emotional intelligence, and teamwork will become increasingly important, as these are areas where humans still have an edge over machines. Employers are already shifting their focus from hiring based on credentials to looking for individuals with the right mind-set and potential to grow within an organisation.

Ultimately, the shift toward education and re-skilling must be seen as part of a broader social transformation. Preparing for the future of work is not just about keeping pace with technology; it is about ensuring that every individual has the opportunity to lead a meaningful and dignified life, regardless of how the labour market evolves. Education in the 21st century should empower people to pursue purpose, not just paycheques. This requires a deep commitment to inclusivity, ensuring that everyone—whether they are in rural Limpopo, urban Johannesburg, or the informal settlements of Cape Town—has access to the knowledge and opportunities they need to thrive in a changing world.

While the challenges are significant, so are the opportunities. The shift toward automation provides a chance to reshape our education system in ways that align more closely with the values of equity, creativity, and lifelong learning. South Africa's future will be shaped not just by the technologies we adopt but by the people we choose to become. Preparing for an automated future is not simply a matter of surviving disruption; it is about envisioning a society where education serves as a foundation for personal growth, collective well-being, and shared prosperity. With the right investments, policies, and partnerships, South Africa can build an education system that equips its people not just to navigate the future of work but to thrive within it.

# 12 Entrepreneurship and innovation: New paths to economic empowerment

In a world where automation continues to displace traditional jobs, entrepreneurship and innovation are emerging as powerful tools for economic empowerment. As more industries become automated and fewer jobs remain in their current form, starting a business or engaging in creative problem-solving offers a viable path for individuals to regain control over their livelihoods. For South Africans, this shift holds both great promise and significant challenges. The entrepreneurial spirit has always been present across the country—from street vendors and township businesses to tech start-ups and social enterprises—but unleashing its full potential in an automated future requires a deliberate focus on fostering innovation and supporting those who take the leap.

At its core, entrepreneurship is about creating value by identifying opportunities and solving problems. In a country like South Africa, where unemployment remains stubbornly high and inequality deeply entrenched, innovation has the potential to unlock new economic opportunities. The pressing challenges faced by communities—whether they involve access to healthcare, education, or sustainable energy—can also be catalysts for local solutions. With the right resources and support, ordinary citizens can harness these challenges as opportunities to develop innovative products and services that benefit their communities and generate income. Entrepreneurship, in this sense, is not limited to starting companies for profit; it is also about driving social change and creating meaningful work that aligns with personal purpose.

However, becoming an entrepreneur in South Africa is no easy task. Many aspiring business owners face significant barriers, including limited access to funding, mentorship, and markets. While automation opens up new possibilities for innovation, it also introduces greater competition, not only locally but from global players. Entrepreneurs must learn to navigate a rapidly changing landscape, where technological advancements can render business models obsolete almost overnight. For those with the ambition to start their own businesses, the pressure to constantly innovate can be daunting. Yet, this very uncertainty offers an opportunity to reframe failure as part of the entrepreneurial journey—something to learn from, rather than fear. Developing resilience and adaptability is crucial for navigating the unpredictable nature of entrepreneurship in the age of automation.

Technology, paradoxically, plays both a disruptive and an empowering role. On one hand, automation threatens traditional jobs; on the other, it provides tools that can reduce the barriers to starting and growing businesses. Digital platforms now make it easier for entrepreneurs to reach customers, manage operations, and access resources. Social media, e-commerce platforms, and payment gateways enable small businesses to operate more efficiently and reach wider audiences than ever before. The rise of the gig economy also offers new avenues for self-employment, allowing individuals to earn income through flexible, task-based work. While these opportunities are not without their challenges—particularly regarding job security and income volatility—they offer a glimpse into how entrepreneurship is evolving in response to technological change.

Encouraging entrepreneurship as a pathway to economic empowerment also requires shifting mind-sets. Many South Africans, particularly young people, have been conditioned to view employment in traditional sectors as the only route to financial stability and social status. Breaking away from this mind-set involves reimagining what work and success look like in the 21st century. Entrepreneurship needs to be seen as a legitimate and valuable career path, not a last resort for those unable to find formal employment. This shift will require support from multiple stakeholders, including schools, universities, and government institutions. Education systems, in particular, must evolve to nurture creativity, critical thinking, and problem-solving skills—traits that are essential for entrepreneurship but often overlooked in traditional curricula.

Mentorship also plays a critical role in the success of entrepreneurs. Having access to experienced mentors who can provide guidance, share insights, and open doors to opportunities can make a significant difference in the early stages of a business. South Africa has several incubators, accelerators, and innovation hubs dedicated to supporting start-ups, but these resources are often concentrated in urban centres like Johannesburg and Cape Town, leaving rural entrepreneurs at a disadvantage. Expanding access to these resources is essential if entrepreneurship is to become a truly inclusive force for economic empowerment. Initiatives that connect aspiring business owners with mentors and investors—whether through online platforms or community networks—can help level the playing field and ensure that innovation thrives across the country.

Government and corporate policies must also align to create an enabling environment for entrepreneurship. While there are already several programmes aimed at promoting small business development, more can be done to address the structural barriers that entrepreneurs face. Access to finance remains a major hurdle, particularly for young entrepreneurs and those from marginalised backgrounds. Traditional banks are often reluctant to lend to start-ups without established track records or collateral, which makes it difficult for many entrepreneurs to get their ideas off the ground.

Expanding access to alternative forms of funding—such as venture capital, angel investors, and crowd-funding platforms—will be critical in fostering innovation.

At the same time, corporate South Africa has a role to play in supporting entrepreneurship through procurement policies that prioritise small and emerging businesses. Large companies can help create opportunities by including start-ups in their supply chains, providing market access, and offering mentorship or partnership opportunities. Government, too, can incentivise innovation through targeted tax breaks, grants, and subsidies aimed at encouraging entrepreneurship in sectors with high growth potential. Supporting small businesses is not just about creating jobs; it is about building a more diverse and resilient economy, where innovation flourishes and opportunities are available to all.

The informal sector also deserves recognition as a vital part of South Africa's entrepreneurial ecosystem. From spaza shops and hair salons to street food vendors, informal businesses play a crucial role in sustaining livelihoods and providing essential services in communities. While these businesses may not fit the conventional definition of entrepreneurship, they embody the same spirit of resourcefulness and determination. As automation reshapes the economy, finding ways to support informal entrepreneurs—through training, access to credit, and infrastructure improvements—will be key to ensuring that no one is left behind.

In the end, entrepreneurship and innovation offer more than just economic empowerment; they provide individuals with a sense of purpose and agency in a world where the future of work is increasingly uncertain. Starting a business is not simply about making money—it is about creating something meaningful, taking risks, and having the freedom to shape one's own path. Innovation, in turn, is not confined to technology; it is a way of thinking that embraces change, challenges the status quo, and seeks out new possibilities. As South Africa navigates the transition to an automated future, fostering entrepreneurship and innovation will be essential for building a society where everyone has the opportunity to contribute, create, and thrive.

In a world where automation threatens to widen economic divides, entrepreneurship offers a way to bridge the gap. It allows individuals to take control of their futures, create jobs for others, and solve problems in ways that benefit society as a whole. But realising this potential requires more than just enthusiasm and ambition—it demands a supportive ecosystem that nurtures ideas, reduces barriers, and encourages resilience. If South Africa can rise to this challenge, entrepreneurship and innovation may well become the pillars of a new economy—one that is not defined by job titles or fixed roles but by the ability to adapt, create, and contribute meaningfully to society. In the face of uncertainty, these qualities will be the key to unlocking economic empowerment for generations to come.

# Part 4: Navigating the Transition

# THE END OF WORK

# 13 Policy responses: Government strategies for mitigating automation's impact

Governments around the world are increasingly faced with the reality that automation is reshaping industries and altering the nature of work at a pace that is difficult to manage. In South Africa, where unemployment is already alarmingly high and inequality runs deep, the impact of automation presents an urgent policy challenge. The threat is not only to jobs but also to social stability. Without proper intervention, automation could exacerbate economic divides and deepen the already fragile relationship between the government and its citizens. Crafting policies to mitigate the impact of automation requires foresight, coordination, and a willingness to break away from outdated models of economic management.

The first step towards effective policy response lies in acknowledging the scope and scale of the challenge. South Africa's government needs to recognise that automation is not just about robots taking over factory jobs. It touches every sector, from mining and agriculture to finance and healthcare. Even jobs that were once considered safe due to their reliance on human creativity or emotional intelligence are no longer immune. The increasing capabilities of artificial intelligence (AI) mean that many administrative, legal, and customer service roles are now at risk. The old playbook of waiting for economic trends to stabilise will no longer work—decisive and proactive intervention is needed to prepare the country for this transformation.

One of the key policy strategies involves prioritising education and re-skilling. The government must invest in education systems that are adaptable and forward-looking, focusing not just on traditional subjects but also on digital literacy, coding, and problem-solving skills. Technical and vocational education and training (TVET) institutions have a particularly important role to play in bridging the skills gap. However, it is not enough to focus only on young learners entering the workforce. Policies must also support mid-career workers through lifelong learning initiatives, ensuring they have access to new skills and can transition into industries that are less susceptible to automation. Establishing partnerships between government, industry, and educational institutions will be essential in aligning training programmes with the evolving needs of the labour market.

Another policy lever involves social safety nets. With job displacement becoming more common, the government must rethink how it supports individuals during periods of unemployment or career transition. Traditional unemployment benefits may need to be expanded, not just in terms of duration but also in scope, to include support for re-training. Some countries are already experimenting with Universal Basic Income (UBI) as a way to cushion the blow of automation. While the idea of UBI remains controversial in South Africa, it is worth serious consideration, given the country's high levels of poverty and unemployment. A guaranteed income would provide a safety net for those left behind by automation, allowing them to pursue new opportunities without the constant fear of destitution.

The government must also foster an environment that encourages entrepreneurship and innovation. As automation disrupts established industries, new opportunities will emerge in areas such as green energy, healthcare technology, and e-commerce. Creating a policy framework that reduces red tape and provides incentives for start-ups will be essential. This includes improving access to funding for small businesses, especially for entrepreneurs from historically disadvantaged backgrounds. Government procurement policies could be designed to favour local innovators, ensuring that small businesses have access to public-sector contracts. In addition, innovation hubs and incubators need to be expanded beyond urban centres like Johannesburg and Cape Town to reach entrepreneurs in rural areas, ensuring that the benefits of automation are distributed more equitably.

Labour market policies must also evolve in response to automation. Rather than focusing solely on protecting existing jobs, the government should promote job-sharing schemes and shorter workweeks, as has been trialled in some European countries. These models allow workers to retain employment while creating space for more people to participate in the economy. South Africa's policy framework needs to shift from an obsession with job quantity to a focus on job quality—ensuring that the work people do is meaningful and sustainable, even if it takes different forms from traditional full-time employment. Policymakers should explore ways to support the gig economy and freelance workers, who are likely to play an increasingly important role in the labour market. Ensuring that these workers have access to benefits such as health insurance and pensions will be key to building an inclusive economy.

At the same time, social dialogue between government, businesses, and labour unions will become more important than ever. South Africa's unions have historically been resistant to technological changes that threaten jobs, and rightly so, given the country's history of inequality and exploitation. However, automation is not a trend that can be stopped—it must be managed in ways that protect workers' rights while embracing the opportunities that technology offers. Government-led discussions can help to build consensus on how best to navigate the transition. These dialogues need to move beyond mere rhetoric, resulting in concrete agreements on retraining programmes, job transitions, and fair compensation for workers affected by automation.

Tax policy will also need to be rethought. As automation reduces the need for human labour, the government may find itself grappling with shrinking income tax revenues. Some countries have already begun exploring the idea of taxing companies based on their use of robots or AI systems. While this approach remains controversial, it raises important questions about how governments will fund public services in the future. South Africa will need to explore creative ways to generate revenue, including wealth taxes or levies on large corporations that benefit the most from automation. These funds can be reinvested into social programmes, education, and infrastructure development to ensure that the benefits of automation are shared more broadly.

The environmental implications of automation must also be considered. Automation offers an opportunity to transition towards more sustainable industries, reducing reliance on resource-intensive practices. For example, automated systems in agriculture can promote precision farming, minimising water usage and reducing the need for harmful pesticides. However, automation also has the potential to increase energy consumption, particularly in data centres and manufacturing. Government policies must strike a balance, encouraging the adoption of green technologies while regulating industries to ensure that environmental sustainability is not sacrificed in the pursuit of economic efficiency.

Ultimately, the success of policy responses will depend on the government's ability to act swiftly and decisively. The pace of technological change leaves little room for complacency. Policymakers must be willing to experiment, adapt, and learn from global best practices while tailoring solutions to South Africa's unique social and economic context. Automation, like any disruptive force, brings both risks and opportunities. If managed well, it has the potential to drive innovation, reduce drudgery, and improve quality of life. However, without proactive policy intervention, the transition could result in widespread social dislocation and increased inequality.

South Africa finds itself at a crossroads. The decisions made in the coming years will determine whether the country emerges stronger and more resilient in the face of automation or whether it becomes a victim of technological change. The task ahead is not just about protecting jobs but about reimagining what work means in the 21st century. The government has a critical role to play in leading this transformation—crafting policies that ensure automation benefits everyone, not just a privileged few. By embracing innovation, investing in people, and fostering social cohesion, South Africa can turn the challenge of automation into an opportunity for growth and renewal. The future of work may be uncertain, but with the right policies in place, it is a future that can be shaped for the better.

# 14 Corporate responsibility: Business leaders' role in managing change

As automation reshapes industries and the nature of employment, businesses stand at the forefront of this transformation. For many organisations, automation is seen as a necessary strategy for efficiency, productivity, and competitiveness. Yet, in the pursuit of profit and innovation, there is a risk of leaving workers behind—creating deep inequalities and social instability. It is in this delicate balancing act that corporate responsibility becomes critical. Business leaders must take accountability not only for the economic outcomes of automation but also for its social and human consequences. They are uniquely positioned to lead with empathy, foresight, and ethical responsibility in this time of radical change, playing an essential role in managing transitions towards a more inclusive future.

Corporate responsibility begins with a mind-set shift—acknowledging that businesses are not isolated entities existing solely to generate profit but are integral parts of society. The actions they take, especially as they integrate artificial intelligence (AI), robotics, and other automated technologies, have far-reaching effects on employees, customers, and communities. Leaders must think beyond quarterly profits and focus on sustainable long-term strategies. This requires building businesses that prioritise people and planet alongside technological innovation. It means engaging with questions of fairness, dignity, and justice in a world where machines are increasingly replacing human labour.

One of the most urgent responsibilities for businesses is ensuring that workers are not abandoned in the transition to automation. While job displacement is an inevitable consequence, companies can minimise its negative impact by adopting fair retrenchment practices. Business leaders must commit to transparent communication with employees about upcoming changes, avoiding sudden layoffs that leave workers in crisis. Early engagement, honest discussions about the future, and providing adequate notice are vital in managing these transitions. Employees need to feel respected and valued, even when their roles are no longer needed.

Offering comprehensive retraining and reskilling programmes is another area where corporate responsibility must be demonstrated. Automation may render certain tasks obsolete, but it also creates new opportunities. Forward-thinking businesses recognise that investing in their workforce's development is not only ethical but also strategic. Reskilling initiatives empower employees to transition into new roles within or outside the organisation. For example, a factory worker whose job is replaced by a robot could be trained to operate and maintain that same robot. Businesses that invest in their workers' future capabilities are more likely to foster loyalty, boost morale, and maintain a positive reputation.

Job-sharing and phased transitions are practical solutions that business leaders can implement to cushion the impact of automation. Instead of immediately replacing a workforce, companies can introduce automation gradually, allowing time for employees to adjust. Job-sharing arrangements, where automation takes over routine tasks while workers focus on higher-value activities, can enhance productivity while preserving employment. Companies that take a collaborative approach to automation not only gain operational benefits but also demonstrate that they value their people's contributions beyond economic metrics.

Leaders must also think creatively about how to harness automation to enhance job quality rather than merely cut costs. Automation can liberate workers from repetitive, dangerous, or physically demanding tasks, allowing them to focus on more meaningful aspects of their work. In healthcare, for instance, automation can handle administrative tasks, freeing up healthcare professionals to spend more time with patients. However, this requires intentional planning—businesses must design roles that integrate automation in ways that enrich, rather than diminish, human labour.

Corporate responsibility extends beyond the immediate workforce to the broader ecosystem of suppliers, customers, and communities. Large businesses, particularly multinationals, must be mindful of how automation affects the supply chains and small businesses that depend on them. When companies automate production or move towards AI-powered systems, they can disrupt smaller suppliers that rely on manual labour. Ethical leaders need to engage with their suppliers and find ways to support them through these transitions, ensuring that automation benefits flow throughout the entire value chain.

Communities where businesses operate are also deeply affected by automation. In areas where a factory or office serves as a major employer, sudden job losses can destabilise the local economy. Responsible business leaders must engage with municipalities and community organisations, working together to develop strategies that mitigate social disruptions. This could involve contributing to local development funds, investing in education initiatives, or supporting entrepreneurship programmes that empower displaced workers to create their own opportunities.

The role of business in mental health and well-being cannot be overstated. The psychological toll of job loss, uncertainty, and economic insecurity is immense. Business leaders have a duty to provide mental health support to employees undergoing transitions, whether through counselling services, stress management workshops, or peer support networks. A compassionate approach helps reduce the stigma around mental health, encouraging employees to seek help when they need it. This not only benefits workers but also fosters a healthier and more productive workplace environment.

In addition to supporting employees, businesses must advocate for fair labour practices in a world increasingly dominated by gig and freelance work. Automation often drives companies to outsource tasks to gig workers or independent contractors, creating a workforce that operates without traditional job security or benefits. Responsible leaders must champion new labour models that protect the rights and well-being of gig workers, ensuring access to basic benefits like healthcare, pensions, and paid leave. This will require innovative partnerships with government and labour unions to develop frameworks that align with the realities of the modern economy.

Transparency and accountability are essential elements of corporate responsibility in the age of automation. Business leaders must be transparent about the motivations behind their adoption of automated technologies, sharing data on how these changes affect employment and productivity. Companies that openly discuss their automation strategies foster trust with employees, customers, and stakeholders. Accountability mechanisms, such as public reports on workforce impact or independent audits, can help businesses maintain integrity and avoid accusations of exploitation.

Diversity and inclusion should also be central to any responsible automation strategy. Businesses must ensure that automation does not disproportionately affect marginalised groups, such as women, youth, or people with disabilities. Leaders should actively monitor the impact of automation on diversity within their organisations, taking steps to address imbalances and ensure equal access to new opportunities. Creating inclusive workplaces not only aligns with corporate values but also unlocks the potential of a broader talent pool.

Responsible businesses must also engage with environmental sustainability in their automation strategies. While automation promises greater efficiency, it can also drive higher energy consumption, particularly in industries like manufacturing and data processing. Business leaders have a responsibility to minimise their environmental impact, whether by adopting green technologies, investing in renewable energy, or offsetting their carbon footprint. Automation must align with sustainability goals, contributing to a greener economy rather than exacerbating climate challenges.

Collaboration between businesses, government, and civil society is crucial for managing the complex transitions that automation brings. No single sector can address the challenges alone. Business leaders must engage in policy dialogues, contributing their expertise to help shape regulations that promote fair automation practices. Participating in public-private partnerships can enhance the impact of training programmes, job creation initiatives, and community development projects, ensuring that automation benefits society as a whole.

In addition to collaboration, businesses must embrace a culture of continuous learning and innovation. Automation is not a one-off change but a continuous process of adaptation. Responsible leaders foster a mind-set of lifelong learning within their organisations, encouraging employees to embrace change and develop new skills. Companies that prioritise innovation remain resilient in the face of disruption, positioning themselves to thrive in a rapidly changing economy.

At the heart of corporate responsibility is the recognition that businesses have a duty to uphold human dignity, even in a world increasingly shaped by machines. Automation must not be used as a tool for dehumanisation but rather as an opportunity to reimagine work in ways that empower individuals and communities. Business leaders who act with empathy, integrity, and foresight can ensure that the transition to automation is a just and inclusive one, where technological progress serves the greater good.

The future of work will be defined by the choices made today. Business leaders have a unique opportunity to shape that future by embracing corporate responsibility in all its dimensions. By prioritising people, fostering inclusion, and building sustainable communities, businesses can help create a world where automation enhances, rather than diminishes, human identity. The journey towards that future will not be easy, but it is one that responsible leaders must embark on with courage and conviction.

# 15 Community initiatives: Local solutions for a global problem

In a world increasingly dominated by automation, many of the most pressing challenges cannot be solved through national policy or corporate strategy alone. Community-driven initiatives offer powerful, grassroots solutions to the disruptions brought by automation. It is in local spaces—neighbourhoods, cooperatives, and small enterprises—where human connection thrives, new opportunities emerge, and the resilience needed to face global change is built. When automation threatens jobs, identity, and mental well-being, local communities can foster social bonds, shared purpose, and support networks that counteract isolation and economic hardship. These efforts remind us that even in the shadow of technological shifts, people and communities remain the bedrock of society.

One of the most immediate responses to job losses caused by automation is the creation of community-led retraining programmes. These initiatives focus on equipping residents with new skills, often aligning with the needs of the local economy. In places where industries have automated, community centres offer courses in areas like IT support, coding, and entrepreneurship. Unlike large-scale government programmes that can feel distant and impersonal, local initiatives provide training in a more supportive, familiar environment. They understand the unique challenges of their communities and tailor solutions to fit local realities, allowing people to regain confidence and purpose.

Community initiatives also promote inclusive employment by creating work opportunities that embrace social enterprises and cooperatives. Across South Africa, we've seen initiatives where communities come together to build businesses that prioritise people over profit. From agricultural cooperatives to small craft industries, these projects provide work while ensuring that economic gains remain within the community. As automation takes over mainstream sectors, cooperatives offer alternative ways of working that are rooted in collaboration and shared ownership, fostering a sense of belonging and collective achievement.

One example of local innovation can be found in urban farming projects. In cities where automation has led to widespread unemployment, these initiatives not only address food insecurity but also provide meaningful work. Rooftop gardens, community plots, and vertical farming projects bring people together to grow produce for sale or local consumption. Beyond providing jobs, urban farms cultivate skills, environmental awareness, and social cohesion. They offer a powerful counter-narrative to the dehumanisation that automation can bring, reconnecting people to nature and each other.

Informal economies also play a crucial role in communities navigating the disruptions of automation. Street vendors, market traders, and spaza shop owners make up an essential part of local economies, especially in townships and rural areas. Community initiatives often focus on supporting these micro-entrepreneurs, offering access to finance, training, and resources. These efforts help sustain livelihoods where formal employment is no longer accessible, empowering individuals to create their own income streams in a way that aligns with their community's needs.

Community-based organisations also tackle the mental health challenges that arise from job displacement and economic insecurity. Local support groups, wellness workshops, and peer counselling networks create spaces where people can share their struggles and find strength in solidarity. Unlike corporate wellness programmes, which can feel disconnected from real-life experiences, these community-led efforts are grounded in empathy and shared experience. They understand the cultural and social dynamics of their areas and offer support in ways that are accessible and meaningful to participants.

Art, music, and cultural initiatives offer another powerful response to the identity crisis caused by automation. Community art centres, theatre groups, and music collectives provide platforms for self-expression, creativity, and storytelling. These projects remind people of their intrinsic worth beyond the confines of work. When automation threatens to reduce human value to economic productivity, the arts celebrate the richness of human experience. Cultural initiatives foster pride, resilience, and joy—qualities that are essential for communities facing uncertain futures.

Local entrepreneurship hubs play a pivotal role in nurturing innovation and economic resilience. These hubs provide shared workspaces, mentorship, and networking opportunities for small businesses and start-ups. They bring together entrepreneurs, creatives, and community leaders to collaborate on solutions that address local challenges. By fostering innovation from the ground up, these hubs not only create jobs but also empower people to reimagine work in ways that align with their passions and skills.

In areas where automation disrupts access to education, community initiatives fill critical gaps. Libraries, after-school programmes, and tutoring groups ensure that children and youth continue to learn, even when schools are under-resourced. In some cases, community organisations develop alternative education models that emphasise practical skills, creativity, and critical thinking—qualities that remain essential in an automated world. These initiatives ensure that the next generation is prepared for the future, with the confidence to navigate change and uncertainty.

Community-based renewable energy projects offer a glimpse of how local solutions can address global problems. In regions where automation impacts traditional industries, such as mining or manufacturing, communities are turning to solar, wind, and hydroelectric power to create new opportunities. These projects not only provide sustainable energy but also create jobs in installation, maintenance, and management. They offer a way for communities to transition towards greener economies while retaining control over their resources and future.

Collaboration between community organisations, businesses, and government is essential for scaling local solutions. Public-private partnerships provide resources, expertise, and support that enable community initiatives to thrive. When businesses invest in local projects and government policies align with community needs, sustainable change becomes possible. These partnerships ensure that automation's benefits are shared more equitably, promoting social and economic inclusion.

Community sports initiatives offer yet another avenue for fostering resilience in the face of automation. Football teams, running clubs, and recreational leagues bring people together, promoting physical health and social connection. In many cases, sports programmes go beyond recreation—they provide mentoring, leadership development, and a sense of purpose for young people. When work is no longer the primary source of identity, sports offer a valuable alternative, nurturing self-esteem, teamwork, and community pride.

Faith-based organisations also play a vital role in communities grappling with the changes brought by automation. Churches, mosques, temples, and other places of worship offer not only spiritual guidance but also practical support. They provide food parcels, counselling services, and safe spaces where people can connect and find hope. Faith communities foster compassion and solidarity, reminding individuals that they are not alone in their struggles.

Environmental stewardship is another area where community initiatives offer solutions to global challenges. From clean-up campaigns to reforestation projects, these initiatives engage residents in activities that restore the natural environment. In doing so, they create opportunities for meaningful work, reconnecting people to the land and instilling a sense of purpose. These efforts remind us that automation must align with environmental sustainability to build a better future for all.

Community initiatives also play a role in bridging the digital divide. In many areas, access to technology remains limited, exacerbating inequalities as automation advances. Local projects that provide free Wi-Fi, computer literacy classes, and access to devices ensure that residents are not left behind. These efforts empower people to participate in the digital economy, unlocking new opportunities for learning, work, and social connection.

Housing cooperatives and community land trusts offer solutions to the displacement that often accompanies automation. In urban areas where automation changes the economic landscape, rising property prices can push residents out. Community-led housing initiatives ensure that people remain rooted in their neighbourhoods, preserving social networks and cultural identity. These efforts demonstrate that communities can take control of their futures, creating spaces where everyone has a place to belong.

Local storytelling initiatives capture and preserve the experiences of people navigating the changes brought by automation. Oral history projects, community publications, and digital archives document the voices of those affected by technological shifts. These stories provide valuable insights into the human impact of automation, ensuring that future generations understand the challenges and triumphs of this era.

Volunteerism also plays a crucial role in fostering community resilience. In times of crisis, people come together to support one another through acts of kindness and service. Whether through food drives, mentorship programmes, or neighbourhood watch groups, volunteers demonstrate the power of collective action. These initiatives remind us that even in an automated world, human connection remains invaluable.

Ultimately, community initiatives offer hope in a time of profound change. They remind us that while automation may reshape industries, it cannot replace the human spirit. By working together, communities can create new opportunities, foster resilience, and build a future that is inclusive and just. The solutions to global problems may not always come from the top—but from the ground up, in the everyday efforts of people determined to build a better world.

# 16 Personal Resilience – Strategies for Adapting to an Uncertain Future

In a world where technological change is unfolding at an unprecedented pace, personal resilience is becoming more critical than ever. Automation, artificial intelligence (AI), and machine learning are reshaping industries, rendering traditional skills obsolete and making uncertainty a daily reality. In this environment, personal resilience—the ability to adapt, recover, and grow in the face of challenges—becomes not just a desirable trait but an essential one. South Africans, like people worldwide, must equip themselves with mental, emotional, and practical strategies to thrive in a future where automation disrupts conventional career paths. This chapter explores how individuals can build resilience to navigate the shifting landscape of work and identity.

At the heart of resilience lies the ability to reframe challenges as opportunities for growth. Job losses and career shifts—although painful—can open doors to new beginnings. However, such a mind-set is not automatic. It requires conscious effort and self-reflection. Resilient individuals actively work on understanding that failure and setbacks are part of life's journey. Whether it is retraining after job displacement or starting a new business, reframing difficulties as learning experiences can shift focus from despair to hope. Resilience is not about avoiding hardship but about finding strength in it.

One of the most powerful tools in building personal resilience is emotional self-regulation. In uncertain times, it is easy to feel overwhelmed by fear, anxiety, and frustration. However, resilient people learn to manage their emotional responses, recognising that these feelings, while valid, do not have to dictate their actions. Practices such as mindfulness and journaling help individuals process their emotions in healthy ways. In South Africa, where unemployment and inequality already contribute to high levels of stress, emotional self-regulation will be essential in coping with automation's disruptions. Developing emotional resilience will equip individuals to face setbacks with clarity and calmness, helping them make thoughtful decisions in the midst of change.

Resilience also involves building a mind-set of continuous learning. Automation will demand new skills, and those who are adaptable learners will be best positioned to succeed. Embracing lifelong learning—whether through formal education, online courses, or personal development workshops—ensures that individuals remain competitive in a changing job market. In South Africa, where access to education is often unequal, a commitment to self-improvement becomes even more critical. It may require tapping into free resources, joining learning communities, or seeking mentorship opportunities. Those who take ownership of their learning journey will be better prepared to navigate the evolving world of work.

Social support networks are a vital source of

resilience. No one can build resilience in isolation. Having a circle of friends, family, or colleagues to lean on during difficult times provides emotional support and practical assistance. In South African culture, where the spirit of *Ubuntu*—the belief that our shared humanity connects us—plays a central role, fostering community connections can help individuals manage change. Reaching out for support, whether through professional counselling or informal conversations, can make the difference between feeling isolated and finding strength in solidarity. Resilient people know that it is okay to ask for help and that mutual support is a key part of overcoming adversity.

Developing a sense of purpose is another cornerstone of resilience. Automation threatens to disrupt the traditional ways in which people derive meaning from work. However, those who cultivate purpose beyond their jobs—whether through volunteering, hobbies, or involvement in their communities—can find fulfilment even in uncertain times. Purpose provides a sense of direction and helps individuals maintain motivation when faced with setbacks. In South Africa, where many people already engage in community-driven initiatives, finding purpose through contribution to the greater good can be a powerful way to stay resilient in the face of change.

Physical well-being also plays a crucial role in building resilience. A healthy body supports a healthy mind, and individuals who maintain good physical health are better equipped to handle stress and challenges. Regular exercise, balanced nutrition, and adequate sleep are foundational habits that support mental and emotional resilience. Automation's impact may create stress and uncertainty, but caring for one's physical health can provide stability amidst disruption. Resilient people understand that their well-being is interconnected and take proactive steps to maintain balance in all areas of their lives.

Financial resilience is increasingly important in an automated future where traditional job security may be hard to come by. Developing good financial habits, such as saving, budgeting, and reducing debt, can provide a buffer against economic shocks. Automation may create instability in the labour market, but individuals who are financially prepared will be better positioned to navigate uncertain periods. In South Africa, where economic inequality is a significant challenge, financial literacy and planning become critical tools for personal resilience. Building financial security, even in small steps, can provide peace of mind and create options in times of change.

Resilience is not just about individual efforts—it also involves fostering a sense of agency and self-empowerment. In uncertain times, it is easy to feel powerless, but resilient people take proactive steps to shape their own futures. This might involve exploring new career paths, starting a business, or participating in community initiatives. In South Africa, where entrepreneurship is often celebrated as a pathway to empowerment, fostering a spirit of agency will be essential for individuals to thrive in the face of automation. Resilient people understand that while they cannot control every outcome, they can control their responses and actions.

Another key aspect of resilience is the ability to adapt to change. Automation will likely introduce new ways of working, and individuals who are flexible and open to change will have a significant advantage. This might involve embracing remote work, freelancing, or participating in the gig economy. In South Africa, where traditional employment is already under pressure, being open to unconventional work arrangements will be an important part of personal resilience. Resilient people are those who can shift their mind-set and embrace change as an opportunity rather than a threat.

Ultimately, resilience is a journey, not a destination. It is a process of continuous growth, learning, and adaptation. Automation will undoubtedly challenge individuals, but those who invest in building resilience will find opportunities for personal and professional growth. In South Africa, where communities have long demonstrated resilience in the face of adversity, the lessons learned from past challenges will provide a foundation for navigating the future. Resilient individuals will not only survive in an automated world—they will thrive, finding new ways to create meaning and contribute to society.

In conclusion, building personal resilience in the

face of automation requires a multifaceted approach that includes emotional regulation, lifelong learning, social support, financial planning, and a sense of purpose. While the road ahead may be uncertain, resilience offers a way forward. It empowers individuals to embrace change, overcome setbacks, and find opportunities for growth. In South Africa and beyond, those who cultivate resilience will be best positioned to navigate the challenges of automation and create fulfilling lives in a rapidly changing world. Personal resilience is not just about surviving the future—it is about thriving within it, no matter what changes come our way.

# Part 5: Conclusion

# THE END OF WORK

# 17 Summary of key findings and implications

The journey through this book has highlighted the complex and profound ways in which automation is reshaping the world of work and, by extension, human identity. Technology, once a tool to aid human labour, is now becoming capable of replacing it. From AI-driven systems to autonomous robots, automation is no longer confined to manufacturing floors or coding lines—it is permeating every sector of the economy. The impact is both far-reaching and multifaceted, touching individual lives, communities, and entire nations. This summary distils the key findings of the previous chapters, with a focus on the human implications of a future where work, as we know it, may no longer define us.

The first key finding is that automation's impact is not an abstract or distant threat—it is already happening. Machines are increasingly performing tasks once thought to be the exclusive domain of humans. From cashierless stores to self-driving trucks, these advancements are disrupting industries at a rapid pace. This reality underscores the urgency of preparing for a future where fewer people may be needed to perform traditional jobs, pushing societies into uncharted territory. For South Africa, with its high unemployment rate, this presents both a crisis and an opportunity, as the workforce must pivot towards skills that complement, rather than compete with, automation.

One of the most pressing implications is the displacement of workers. Sectors such as manufacturing, retail, transportation, and even professional services are particularly vulnerable. The rapid adoption of AI-powered systems threatens to eliminate millions of jobs globally, with South Africa not spared. This displacement has the potential to exacerbate existing inequalities, leaving behind those who lack access to new skills or opportunities. The ripple effects could further deepen socio-economic divides, especially in a country where inequality is already stark and unemployment is a persistent challenge.

A recurring theme in this book is the psychological impact of job loss. Work is more than just a means to earn a living—it is deeply intertwined with personal identity, self-worth, and social belonging. The removal of this structure can leave individuals grappling with feelings of purposelessness and anxiety. South African workers, already vulnerable to economic shocks, may experience heightened emotional and mental strain. The loss of work may not just affect individuals but also destabilise family dynamics and erode social cohesion within communities, leading to increased levels of depression and social alienation.

Equally concerning are the economic implications of automation. As more jobs are automated, wage stagnation and unemployment may become entrenched realities. With fewer people earning steady incomes, consumer spending will likely decline, creating a vicious cycle of reduced demand and shrinking economic activity. South Africa's economy, heavily reliant on consumer spending, could face severe challenges. Policy responses will need to address not only job losses but also the erosion of purchasing power, particularly in low-income communities.

The book has also explored the potential of Universal Basic Income (UBI) as a solution to economic insecurity. UBI offers a lifeline by providing individuals with a guaranteed income, enabling them to meet basic needs even in the absence of employment. However, the feasibility of implementing such a scheme in South Africa—given budget constraints and other competing priorities—remains uncertain. While UBI may offer short-term relief, the long-term success of any such initiative will depend on how well it addresses not only economic needs but also the psychological and social aspects of job displacement.

Education and re-skilling emerge as essential components of preparing for an automated future. Workers must be equipped with skills that are in demand in a digital economy, such as data analysis, robotics, and AI programming. However, South

Africa's education system, plagued by structural inequalities and resource shortages, may struggle to meet this demand. The challenge will be to create learning pathways that are accessible to all, ensuring that workers from diverse backgrounds can benefit from new opportunities. Lifelong learning will become a norm, with individuals needing to adapt continuously to technological changes throughout their careers.

Entrepreneurship and innovation present another pathway to economic empowerment. As automation disrupts traditional industries, new business opportunities will emerge, especially in fields related to technology and sustainability. South Africa, with its strong entrepreneurial spirit, is well-positioned to harness this potential. However, entrepreneurs will require support in the form of mentorship, funding, and access to markets. Encouraging a culture of innovation will be key to building an economy that thrives alongside automation rather than being overrun by it.

Throughout the book, the role of government policy has been highlighted as a critical factor in managing the transition to an automated future. Governments will need to craft policies that mitigate the negative impacts of automation while encouraging innovation. In South Africa, policy efforts must focus on reducing inequality, ensuring access to education and re-skilling, and fostering social safety nets. Balancing the interests of workers, businesses, and communities will require nuanced, forward-thinking strategies. Governments must act proactively, rather than reactively, to prevent social unrest and economic decline.

Corporate responsibility also plays an important role in this transition. Business leaders must recognise that automation's benefits cannot come at the expense of human dignity and well-being. Companies will need to invest in their employees, offering opportunities for upskilling and career development. Ethical considerations must guide decisions about automating jobs, ensuring that workers are treated fairly and given the support they need to transition into new roles. Collaboration between the public and private sectors will be essential to ensure that the benefits of automation are shared widely.

At the community level, grassroots initiatives will be crucial in addressing the challenges posed by automation. Local organisations, non-profits, and community leaders can play an active role in supporting displaced workers and fostering social cohesion. In South Africa, where the spirit of *Ubuntu* remains a powerful force, community-based solutions can offer a sense of belonging and purpose to individuals affected by job loss. Strengthening local networks will ensure that no one is left behind in the transition to a new economic landscape.

Personal resilience stands out as a recurring theme throughout this book. Individuals will need to develop coping mechanisms to navigate the uncertainties brought about by automation. Building emotional resilience, cultivating a mind-set of lifelong learning, and developing strong support networks will be essential strategies. In South Africa, where many people have already demonstrated remarkable resilience in the face of adversity, these skills will be invaluable in adapting to a future shaped by technology.

Ultimately, the findings of this book suggest that the future of work will require a fundamental rethinking of what it means to have purpose and identity. As automation continues to redefine industries and professions, individuals and societies will need to find new ways to derive meaning and fulfilment. Work may no longer be the central pillar of identity, but that does not mean that purpose will be lost. Communities, relationships, and personal growth will take on greater significance, offering alternative sources of meaning.

The transition to an automated future will not be easy, and there will be challenges along the way. However, this book also highlights the potential for positive change. If managed thoughtfully, automation can create opportunities for economic empowerment, greater equality, and improved quality of life. The key will be to ensure that technological progress serves humanity rather than undermining it. With proactive policies, ethical business practices, and resilient communities, it is possible to navigate this transition successfully.

In conclusion, the findings of this book underscore the importance of preparing for the challenges and opportunities that automation presents. The future of work may look different from what we are accustomed to, but it need not be bleak. By embracing change with open minds and open hearts, individuals and societies can build a future where technology enhances, rather than diminishes, the human experience. The journey ahead will require courage, creativity, and collaboration, but the potential rewards—both personal and collective—are well worth the effort.

# 18 Call to Action: Collective Responsibility for Shaping the Future

The rise of automation has brought humanity to a crossroads, demanding urgent reflection on what lies ahead. The pace of technological change is relentless, but the future is not predetermined. It is a canvas waiting to be shaped by our collective actions and decisions. This chapter is a call to action—an appeal for people, communities, businesses, and governments to work together towards a future where technology enhances human life rather than eroding it. The challenges posed by automation are immense, but they are not insurmountable. What is required is a shared commitment to building a more inclusive, just, and sustainable world.

We can no longer afford to view the future of work as an issue that only concerns policymakers or business leaders. The transition into a world increasingly governed by automation requires active participation from all sectors of society. Each of us—whether employed or unemployed, young or old, in urban centres or rural villages—has a role to play. This is a moment for communities to come together and confront the realities of technological disruption with a sense of unity and purpose. A passive approach will only leave many behind, deepening existing inequalities and social divisions.

For individuals, this call to action means embracing lifelong learning and personal growth. As traditional jobs disappear or evolve, it becomes essential to develop new skills and adapt to changing work environments. But it's not just about acquiring technical expertise; it's about cultivating resilience, creativity, and emotional intelligence. These are the human traits that machines cannot replicate. In South Africa, where unemployment and inequality already threaten social cohesion, preparing oneself for an uncertain future is not merely a personal responsibility—it is a collective one.

Communities have an equally vital role in navigating this transformation. The concept of *Ubuntu*, the idea that "I am because we are," reminds us that no person can thrive in isolation. Communities must become spaces where displaced workers and marginalised individuals are supported, valued, and empowered. Local initiatives—whether they focus on skills development, entrepreneurship, or mental health support—are critical to ensuring that no one is left behind. By fostering a spirit of solidarity, communities can become anchors of stability and hope during turbulent times.

Businesses, too, bear a significant responsibility. While technological innovation is essential for progress, it should not come at the expense of human dignity. Corporate leaders must recognise that their actions shape not only the bottom line but also the future of society. This means adopting ethical practices, investing in employee upskilling, and creating inclusive work environments where people can thrive alongside technology. In South Africa's context, where inequality runs deep, businesses must step up as agents of positive change, driving sustainable growth that benefits all citizens, not just a privileged few.

Governments, as custodians of public welfare, must play a central role in managing the transition towards an automated future. Public policy has the power to steer technological progress in ways that promote social equity and economic justice. Governments need to invest heavily in education, training, and social safety nets, ensuring that citizens are not left vulnerable to the disruptive forces of automation. In South Africa, this requires bold action—policies that prioritise re-skilling the workforce, supporting small businesses, and addressing the structural inequalities that automation may exacerbate.

However, no government can succeed in isolation. Collaboration between the public and private sectors is essential. South Africa's development will depend on partnerships that leverage the strengths of each sector, creating a shared vision for a future where technology serves humanity. Businesses, civil society organisations, and government agencies must work together to design policies and initiatives that promote economic inclusion, foster innovation, and safeguard the well-being of citizens. Cooperation, rather than competition, will be key to overcoming the challenges of automation.

Education systems will need to be reimagined for a world where lifelong learning becomes the norm. The idea that formal education ends with a degree or diploma is outdated. Schools, universities, and training institutions must prepare students not just for the jobs of today but for those that have yet to be imagined. This requires a shift towards teaching critical thinking, problem-solving, and adaptability—skills that will remain relevant no matter how technology evolves. In South Africa, where access to quality education remains unequal, ensuring that all citizens have the opportunity to learn and grow will be critical.

The social implications of automation demand that we rethink our values and priorities as a society. As machines take over routine tasks, we must ask ourselves: What does it mean to be human? How can we find meaning and purpose beyond work? These are questions that require deep introspection and open dialogue. It is an opportunity to redefine success, moving away from a narrow focus on productivity and consumption towards a more holistic understanding of well-being and happiness. South Africa, with its diverse cultural heritage, has much to offer in this conversation.

Mental health must become a priority as we navigate this uncertain future. The emotional toll of job displacement, financial insecurity, and identity loss cannot be ignored. Support systems—whether through counselling services, peer networks, or community initiatives—will be essential in helping individuals cope with the psychological impact of automation. South Africans, who have shown remarkable resilience in the face of historical challenges, must draw on that strength to confront the emotional challenges posed by the future of work.

While automation brings risks, it also presents opportunities for creating a more sustainable and equitable economy. New industries will emerge, driven by innovation and technological advances. The green economy, for example, offers significant potential for job creation in sectors such as renewable energy, sustainable agriculture, and environmental conservation. South Africa, with its abundant natural resources, can position itself as a leader in these fields. However, realising this potential will require strategic investment and a commitment to long-term planning.

Entrepreneurship will play a crucial role in building the economy of the future. As traditional jobs become scarcer, more people will need to create their own opportunities. Entrepreneurs will need support in the form of mentorship, funding, and access to markets. In South Africa, where many small businesses struggle to survive, fostering a culture of entrepreneurship will be vital. This is not just about economic growth; it is about empowering individuals to take control of their own futures and contribute to society in meaningful ways.

Technology, if used wisely, can also be a force for good. Automation has the potential to improve quality of life by reducing the burden of tedious and dangerous work. It can free up time for individuals to pursue creative, social, and leisure activities. However, realising these benefits will require intentional design—ensuring that technology serves humanity rather than enslaving it. South Africans must engage in conversations about how technology can enhance, rather than diminish, our shared humanity.

The call to action is also a call for inclusion. Automation must not become a tool that widens existing inequalities. Marginalised communities, women, and people with disabilities must be included in the new economic landscape. This means creating opportunities for all citizens to participate in the digital economy and ensuring that technological progress benefits everyone, not just a select few. In South Africa, building an inclusive future will require intentional policies and practices that address systemic inequalities.

Finally, this call to action is a reminder that the future is not something that happens to us—it is something we create together. The decisions we make today will shape the world our children inherit. We have a responsibility to ensure that the next generation inherits a future that is fair, just, and full of possibility. This requires courage, vision, and a commitment to working together for the common good. South Africans have faced many challenges in the past, and with the same spirit of resilience and determination, we can rise to meet the challenges of automation.

The task ahead is not easy, but it is not impossible. By embracing a mind-set of collaboration and collective responsibility, we can shape a future where technology works for humanity, not against it. The road ahead will require us to confront difficult truths, make tough decisions, and rethink long-held assumptions. But it is also a road filled with opportunity—a chance to build a world that is more inclusive, compassionate, and sustainable.

In the end, the future is ours to shape. Each of us has a role to play, and together, we can create a world where automation enhances human potential rather than undermining it. This is the moment to act, to dream, and to build. The future is calling—and it is up to us to answer.

# 19 Epilogue: The Future of Human Identity in an Automated World

The world stands on the precipice of a profound transformation. As automation reshapes industries, economies, and societies, we find ourselves at a critical juncture where the future of human identity must be reimagined. What does it mean to be human when machines take over the tasks we once defined ourselves by? How do we find purpose and dignity in a world where work as we know it may no longer be the central pillar of our existence? These are questions that cannot be answered with simple solutions. They demand reflection, adaptation, and a commitment to reshaping our understanding of identity in ways that align with this new reality.

At the heart of this journey lies the challenge of redefining what it means to belong, to contribute, and to matter in a world where technology continues to take on more responsibilities. For many, work has not just been a way to earn a living—it has been a source of identity, pride, and social connection. As jobs become automated, and many traditional roles disappear, society will need to develop new frameworks that allow people to feel seen, valued, and connected. This will require bold thinking and the willingness to challenge deeply ingrained beliefs about productivity and success.

The threat of automation has the potential to unravel the very fabric of identity, leaving people to wonder what their role is in a world increasingly run by algorithms and machines. But within this challenge also lies an opportunity. The shift away from routine labour could free people from the pressures of monotonous work and open doors to pursuits that are more meaningful and enriching. It is an invitation to explore creativity, nurture relationships, and develop interests that may have been side-lined by the demands of survival. Yet, this transition will not be easy for everyone.

The struggle to adapt will not be felt evenly across societies. In countries like South Africa, where unemployment is already high, and inequality remains a stubborn legacy of the past, the displacement caused by automation could deepen existing divides. For those already marginalised, losing even low-paying jobs could feel like a final blow to their sense of worth and place in the world. This is why the future of human identity must be built on principles of inclusion, fairness, and shared opportunity. No one can be left behind in this new era.

Reimagining identity in a post-work world requires more than individual reflection—it demands systemic change. Education systems will need to evolve to teach not just technical skills but also emotional intelligence, self-awareness, and adaptability. Governments and businesses will need to foster environments where people can explore their potential beyond conventional career paths. If human identity is no longer tethered to job titles and professional achievements, we must create new narratives that celebrate personal growth, community involvement, and well-being.

One of the most significant shifts we must embrace is the idea that identity can be fluid and multifaceted. In a world where people may move between roles—working part-time, engaging in creative projects, volunteering, or caring for loved ones—we need to move away from rigid labels. No longer should identity be confined to a singular definition like "accountant" or "teacher." Instead, people should be encouraged to embrace the many layers of their existence, finding fulfilment in both formal work and personal pursuits.

The rise of automation may also challenge our sense of purpose. For centuries, work has provided structure, routine, and a sense of direction. When that structure begins to dissolve, individuals may experience moments of confusion, anxiety, or even despair. But purpose does not have to disappear along with jobs. It can be found in relationships, creativity, spirituality, learning, and community involvement. The key will be to recognise that purpose is not something external that we chase—it is something we create within ourselves.

Technology, paradoxically, may play a role in helping us reconnect with what it means to be human.

Automation, artificial intelligence, and robotics can handle repetitive tasks, freeing us to focus on areas that require empathy, imagination, and emotional connection. Machines can serve as tools, not replacements—enhancing our ability to care for one another, solve complex social problems, and explore new frontiers of knowledge and experience. But for this to happen, we must be intentional about how we integrate technology into our lives.

The future of human identity will depend heavily on the values we choose to uphold as a society. Will we prioritise material wealth and status, or will we seek meaning and fulfilment in relationships, service, and personal growth? Will we allow automation to divide us, or will we find ways to use technology to build bridges across communities and generations? These choices will shape not only our individual identities but also the collective identity of humanity in this new era.

It is also important to recognise that identity is not something fixed or static. It evolves throughout life, shaped by experiences, challenges, and relationships. The process of losing a job or facing an uncertain future may initially feel like a loss of identity, but it can also be an opportunity for reinvention. This is a moment to ask deep questions about who we are and who we want to become. It is a chance to redefine identity on our terms, not according to societal expectations or economic systems.

As we look ahead, it is clear that the future will require courage and resilience. There will be moments of doubt and fear, as old certainties crumble and new realities take their place. But human beings are remarkably adaptable. We have faced upheavals throughout history—industrial revolutions, wars, pandemics—and each time, we have found ways to rebuild, renew, and grow. The transition to an automated world will be no different, provided we face it with open hearts and minds.

The role of community will become even more important in this new world. People will need spaces where they can connect, share experiences, and find support. Community initiatives, whether focused on arts, education, or mutual aid, will play a crucial role in helping individuals navigate the complexities of a changing world. South Africa, with its rich tradition of communal values, can lead the way in building networks of care and solidarity that support people through this transition.

In the end, the future of human identity will not be defined by the technologies we create but by the ways we choose to live alongside them. Machines may perform tasks more efficiently, but they cannot replace the joy of human connection, the beauty of creative expression, or the depth of shared experiences. These are the things that make us truly human, and they will remain essential no matter how much the world changes.

This epilogue is not just a reflection on what we stand to lose—it is a celebration of what we stand to gain. The end of work as we know it is not the end of meaning, purpose, or identity. It is the beginning of a new chapter in which we are free to explore what it means to live authentically and intentionally. It is a call to embrace change not with fear, but with curiosity and hope.

As we embark on this journey into an automated future, we must remember that identity is not something given to us by the world—it is something we create for ourselves. It is a choice we make every day in the way we think, act, and connect with others. And it is a choice that remains firmly in our hands, no matter how advanced our technologies become.

The future is unwritten, and the story of human identity is still unfolding. It is up to each of us to ensure that it is a story worth telling.

# ABOUT THE AUTHOR

Michael Mokobane is a seasoned Town and Regional Planner and Heritage Practitioner with over seven years of experience in Urban Development, Property and Project Management. Born and raised in South Africa, he holds a Bachelor of Town and Regional Planning from the University of Pretoria and a Master of Philosophy in Heritage Conservation from the University of Cape Town.

Michael's passion for exploring the intersection of technology, economics, and human purpose inspired him to write *The End of Work: Automation's Threat to Human Identity*. In this book, he draws on his background in planning and heritage to ask critical questions about how technological advancements are reshaping not only the workforce but also the essence of what it means to be human in modern society.

Through his writing, Michael seeks to provoke thought and spark meaningful conversations around automation, identity, and the future of work—encouraging readers to engage with these challenges and opportunities in ways that promote resilience, equity, and innovation. His work reflects both a deep concern for the social impacts of disruptive change and an enduring belief in the human spirit's ability to adapt and thrive.

Find out more at
https://www.amazon.com/stores/Michael-Mokobane/author/B0DCJF4TQ2

# OTHER BOOKS BY (AUTHOR)

1. **The Beauty of Africa: A Traveller's Guide to the Continent's Most Breath-taking Places**
2. **Experience the Vibe: A Guide to South Africa's Top Entertainment Spots**
3. **Degrees of Despair: The Struggle of South Africa's Educated Unemployed Youth**
4. **Where are Men?: An outcry of Gender-Based Violence against Women and Children in South Africa**
5. **Fun for All: A Guide to Family-Friendly Entertainment in South Africa**
6. **Spatial Justice: Transforming South Africa's Divided Cities**
7. **Dream Cities: Reimagining South Africa's Urban Future**

Find out more at
https://www.amazon.com/stores/Michael-Mokobane/author/B0DCJF4TQ2

# CAN I ASK A FAVOUR?

If you enjoyed this book or found it helpful, I'd be truly grateful if you could take a moment to leave a short review on Amazon. Your feedback means a lot to me, and I personally read every review to better understand what readers like you need and want, helping me create even more meaningful content.

If you'd like to leave a review then please visit the link below:

https://www.amazon.com/stores/Michael-Mokobane/author/B0DCJF4TQ2

Thanks for your support!